Volume One

FIGHT TO WIN
with
PRAYER
and
PROCLAMATIONS

LIFEWORK PRESS

FIGHT TO WIN
with
PRAYER
and
PROCLAMATIONS

GLORIA GODSON

LIFEWORK PRESS

Fight To Win, With Prayer and Proclamations, Vol 1

LifeWork Ministries, Inc.
P. O. Box 56
Townsend, DE 19734

www.lifeworkministries.org
lifeworkministriesinc@gmail.com

LifeWork Press

© 2021 by Gloria Godson

All rights reserved solely by the author. No part of this book may be reproduced in any form without the permission of the author. For permission requests, contact lifeworkministriesinc@gmail.com.

Unless otherwise indicated, Scripture quotations taken from the Holy Bible, New Living Translation (NLT). Copyright ©1996, 2004, 2007 by Tyndale House Foundation. Used by permission of Tyndale House Publishers, Inc.

Scripture quotations taken from the New King James Version (NKJV)–*public domain*.

Printed in the United States of America.

ISBN: 978-6-6494-5346-9

Dedicated

to

Emmanuel, Timothy, and Rhema

and

my Friend and Partner, Holy Spirit

CONTENTS

Introduction

Chapter 1—The Power of Words..................................11

Chapter 2— Prayer...22

Chapter 3__ Proclamations.......................................39

Chapter 4—Proclamations in History..........................50

Chapter 5—Proclaim the Word!................................52

Afterword...91

INTRODUCTION

I was introduced to the use of proclamations when I was a new Christian in college. I had a mentor who taught me to proclaim Ephesians 6:10-18. I did not fully understand the power of proclamations at the time, but it became a game changer in my life. I quickly realized that proclaiming the word of God built up my faith. I later found that the Bible said precisely that in Romans 10:17, "So faith comes from hearing, that is, hearing the word of God". Proclaiming the word of God changed how I engaged in the spirit. It helped me to boldly take hold of the word of God, mix it with faith in my heart, and launch it forth to achieve the plans and purposes of God for my life. Prayer and proclamations positioned me to win in the battles of life.

Why We Proclaim

Because we are kingdom people! We belong to the kingdom of God. The kingdom was a very important theme for Jesus. It had a prominent, explicit focus in His teachings. In the ESV translation, the "kingdom" is mentioned 126 times in the gospels alone, mostly in Jesus's teachings. The kingdom is God's way of doing things. It is the government and rule of God on the earth.

Jesus came to inaugurate a kingdom, not a democracy. Some of the first words out of His mouth when He began His ministry were, "The kingdom of God has come" (Matthew 4:17, Matthew 10:7, Mark 1:14-15, Luke 4:43, Luke 8:1, Luke 10:9). In the kingdom there is no lack, sickness, bondage, affliction, or limitation. We belong to the kingdom of God, and the laws of the kingdom operates in our lives and governs our affairs.

In a kingdom, kings have authority and their words carry tremendous power. In Revelation 5:10, the Bible says that God has "made us kings and priests... and we shall reign on the earth". Kings rule and exercise authority through the issuance of edicts, decrees, and proclamations. Jesus said, "the kingdom of God is within you" (Luke 17:21). He also taught us to pray, "Your kingdom come, your will be done on earth as it is in heaven." When we make proclamations, we act as kings to call forth and establish the rule, authority, and government of God in the earth.

CHAPTER 1

THE POWER OF WORDS

Words are primarily containers of power. We are introduced to the amazing power of words in the first chapter of the Bible. Genesis chapter 1 is repeatedly punctuated by two sets of three words, "And God said" and, "And God called". And everything that God said or called came into physical manifestation, every single time! By the end of that chapter, the entire universe had been created, by the power of the spoken word. That is how powerful words are! We live in a word created, word directed, and word dominated world. Simply stated, our world was created by words and responds to words. This is why Jesus spoke to a fig tree, and directed us to speak to mountains. All of creation recognizes and responds to the word of the living God!

    We think in words. When we speak, our words produce images in the minds of all who hear them. When you say the word dog, that paints a picture in our minds of the four legged creature we call man's best friend. The more targeted your words are, the more it clarifies and identifies what type of dog - the color, shape, condition, and so on. Someone can draw, sculpt or "create" that specific dog from your description. They can pick that dog out from a room full of dogs, simply based on your words. That is the power of words, to bring into existence, first in the imagination, and then in the physical realm, what is spoken. When we make proclamations, we take hold in the spirit of a specific, identified, territory, thing, person or provision, and compel them to respond to us in the same way that the earth responded to God in Genesis 1. In other words, a proclamation is an authoritative prayer that takes hold of what God has provided through grace, and brings it into physical manifestation. Proclamations make a demand on God's provision.

Just as natural hands touch the physical body, words are the invisible "hands" that reach into the unseen realm and touch the soul and spirit. In John 6:63, Jesus said, "The words I speak to you are spirit and life."

Hebrews 4:12 states:

> The word of God is alive and powerful. It is sharper than the sharpest two edged sword, cutting between soul and spirit, between joint and marrow. It exposes our innermost thoughts and desires.

Words reach into the spirit realm and create the visible out of the invisible. Hebrews 11:3 confirms this truth. It states, "The entire universe was formed at God's command, that what we now see did not come from anything that can be seen". Romans 4:17 explains how God does this. He "calls the things that are not, as though they are", and they become. To illustrate, when God wanted to make Abraham a father, He changed his name, and began to call him what He wanted him to become – father of many nations. And over time, Abraham became the father of many nations. This is the power of words, particularly, God's word. Hebrews 4:2 emphasizes that when we mix the word of God with faith in our hearts, it produces a profit and enriches the lives of those who speak it. If your words are powerful, and they are, can you imagine anything more powerful than speaking the words of Almighty God?

Working Words

Words have a creative mandate and anointing. They are meant to work. In Genesis 1, every word God said, went to work as soon as He said it, and produced tangible results. In the same way, every word you speak is working either for you or against you. Every word you speak is on assignment. They are working words. Once you believe the word in your heart and launch it forth with your mouth, it will not return empty; it will achieve its creative purpose and assignment. It is unstoppable! Words work, or are supposed to. That is why Jesus said that we will give account for every idle or non-working word we speak (Matthew 12:36). So, put your words to work, for you.

Working Word Principles

PRINCIPLE 1: Words Flow From The Heart. The words that come out of your mouth come from what is in your heart; which come from what is on your mind; which in turn, come from what you allow in through your ear gate, eye gate, and mouth gate. Jesus taught that words flow from the heart. He said, "out of the abundance of the heart, the mouth speaks" (Matthew 12:34). Since words flow from thoughts, if you change your thoughts, you will change your words. If you replace your thoughts with God's thoughts, you will transform not only your words, but your entire life! (Romans 12:1-2).

PRINCIPLE 2: Words Are Containers. There are only two things that fill every word you speak - Life or death; blessing or cursing: The Bible states in Proverbs 18:21, "The tongue has the power of life and death." The New living Translation makes it even clearer. It states, "The tongue can bring death or life; those who love to talk will reap the consequences." So, fill your words with life and blessing.

PRINCIPLE 3: To Choose Life, Speak Life. In Deuteronomy 30:19, God said, "See, I have set before you life and death, blessings and curses. Now choose life, so that you and your children may live". How do you choose life? By loving God and speaking words of life. Conversely, you can literally talk yourself to death, by the words you speak. Apostle James laments the wrongful use of words. Our words, said James, is the fruit that shows the condition of the soil of our hearts. He compares the incongruency of using the same mouth to bless and curse, to salt water and fresh water coming from the same spring, a fig tree producing olives, or a grapevine producing figs. James's point is clear. What is in your heart will eventually spill out through your mouth. Just as a fresh water spring cannot produce salt water, so a healthy heart cannot produce words of cursing and death (James 3:3-12). Speak life!

PRINCIPLE 4: Be Careful Who You Let Speak into Your Life. The same two things in your mouth – life or death, blessing or cursing; are the same things in the mouth of every person who speaks into your life - your doctor, family members, TV actors, movie stars, musicians, your pastor and so on. **There are no neutral words.** Whenever a person opens their mouth to speak to you, whether they are your friends, family members, co-workers, or your doctor, their words will minister either life or death, blessing or cursing. This is why it is of critical importance that you jealously guard who you let speak into your life, because their words can kill or breathe life into you; it can sap you of strength or invigorate you, it can bring fear into your life, or fill you will courage and faith.

PRINCIPLE 4: Your Words Determine the Course of Your Life. Your mouth can literally turn your life around! In James 3:3-10. The Bible compares the tongue to the bit in a horse's mouth that turns the animal in one direction or another; or a ship's rudder that turns the ship one way or another. What this means is that your words determine the course of your life. Your words determine whether you are blessed or cursed, whether you live or die; whether you are sick or well; or whether you are poor or rich. You can set or change the course and direction of your life by what you say. So, if you don't like your life today, you can change it, one word at a time.

PRINCIPLE 5: Your Words Determine, Not Only the Direction, But the Outcomes of Your Life: In one of the most astounding verses in the Bible, Jesus said, "Whoever says to this mountain, 'Be removed and be cast into the sea,' and does not doubt in their heart, but believes that what they say will happen, he will have whatever he says" (Mark 11:23-24). In other words, you can, with faith filled words, create the outcomes of your life. In Numbers 14:28, we see this principle play out sadly in the lives of the Israelites. They went about complaining and saying that God brought them out from Egypt to destroy them in the wilderness. They repeatedly spoke death over themselves with their own mouths, until eventually God said to them, "**'As surely as I live, declares the Lord, I will do to you the very thing I heard you say:** In this wilderness your bodies will fall—every one of you twenty years old or more who was counted in the census and who has grumbled against me." They said that they would die in the wilderness, and they did! You will have what you say.

PRINCIPLE 6: My Words Can Create the Future I Want. God our Father created the world with His spoken word. Then He made us in His image and gave us the same creative ability and authority. We can create our world, the same way that God created the earth, by speaking. In Genesis 1:1–3, the Bible says, "In the beginning, God created the heavens and the earth. The earth was without form and empty, and darkness covered the deep waters. And the Spirit of God was hovering over the surface of the waters. Then God said, 'Let there be light,' and there was light."

"Note that the earth was without form and empty, and darkness was over the deep until God began to speak. God didn't say what He saw; rather, He declared what He wanted to see, and as He spoke it forth, it came into being. He said, "Let there be light, and there was light." He continued to speak until He transformed everything in sight. He spoke forth order where there was chaos, light in place of darkness, and He filled the empty earth, sky, and seas with living creatures without number. He spoke until what He saw in the natural matched what He wanted to see." "*Choosing a Life of Victory*", *Godson*. God gave us the same creative power in our mouths to create life or death in our world. God wants to prosper you, but He needs you to agree with Him and speak accordingly.

PRINCIPLE 7: Your Words Are Powerful! The word of God coming out of your mouth, in faith, is the most potent weapon known to man. Study the word, meditate on the word, speak the word, pray the word, and sing the word. Make the word of God personal - put your name in it, and speak it as a personal declaration. Your ears need to hear the sound of your voice speaking the word of God with faith and conviction. Why? Because faith comes by hearing the word of God - Romans 10:17.

PRINCIPLE 8: The Power of Self-Talk. What you believe and say about yourself has the greatest impact on your life more than any other person's words spoken over you. Your words paint a picture of yourself that you carry with you. They create an internal image of yourself, that is critical to your success or failure. This internal image can either propel and empower you, or deflate and defeat you. Knowing this, you can deploy the power of self-talk to your advantage. You can cancel every curse or negative words spoken over you, and speak life and blessing over yourself.

A Tower to Nowhere

A story in the Bible illustrates the incredible power of words to achieve the impossible! In this story, God Himself said that it is "impossible" to stop a course of action that human beings had set for themselves through the spoken word. God's only option to shut down their operation, was to confuse their language.

Genesis 11:1-9 reports:

> At one time all the people of the world spoke the same language and used the same words. As the people migrated to the east, they found a plain in the land of Babylonia and settled there. They began saying to each other, "Let's make bricks and harden them with fire." (In this region bricks were used instead of stone, and tar was used for mortar.) Then they said, "Come, let's build a great city for ourselves with a tower that reaches into the sky. This will make us famous and keep us from being scattered all over the world." But the LORD came down to look at the city and the tower the people were building. "Look!" he said. "The people are united, and they all speak the same language. After this, nothing they set out to do will be impossible for them! Come, let's go down and confuse the people with different languages. Then they won't be able to understand each other." In that way, the LORD scattered them all over the world, and they stopped building the city. That is why the city was called Babel, because that is where the LORD confused the people with different languages. In this way he scattered them all over the world.

Think about it! The people said, "let's build a great city for ourselves with a tower that reaches into the sky." God saw what they were building and said, "The people are united, and they all speak the same language.... nothing they set out to do will be impossible for them! Come, let's go down and confuse the people with different languages. Then they won't be able to understand each other."

The name of God in this passage is YHWH. This is the personal name of God. It describes the self-existing, eternal God. The first use of this name was in Genesis 2:4, when the Bible summarized the account of creation. So, this name describes the Lord, the creator of heaven and earth. And He said it was impossible to stop mankind from a determined course, set in motion by their words! To stop them, God confused their language, so they could not understand each other. This is the power of words, your words! Can you imagine what will happen when you deploy this unstoppable power of your words to work for you.

Hung By Your Tongue

The devil and the world system have twisted, corrupted and polluted speech, such that the common vernacular used in everyday speech has a death orientation. Routine speech has progressively become ingrained with the devil's pattern, world view, and organizing principle of fear, selfishness, death, and destruction. People say things like, "I am scared to death", "you make me sick", "my leg is killing me", and so on. Even positive things like expressions of love, have become twisted in speech, for example, people say, "I love her to death" or "I love him to pieces". When people laugh heartily at a joke; they say, "You are killing me". Whereas the Bible says the exact opposite, that laughter is good like medicine. The only reason people don't keel over and die immediately when they make these types of statements, is because they don't truly believe it in their hearts.

Likewise, people unwittingly curse themselves by their words. When you say things like, "I can't do anything right", "I am so clumsy", "I am so stupid", "my business is collapsing", "I am the black sheep of the family", "I always mess things up", and so on, you literally curse yourself and hinder your own growth and progress.

Similarly, you can maintain sickness in your life by your words. When you refer to a disease as, "my cancer" or "my shingles" or my Crone's disease" and so on, you claim ownership of the sickness and make room for it in your thinking. The Bible teaches that God wants you to be well, and has made provision for your health and healing. "The health of your body is so important that Jesus paid dearly for it. Isaiah 53:5 and 1 Peter 2:24 says, that by the horrendous stripes that tore His back to shreds, you were, and are healed. So, Jesus fully paid for your health on the cross, but God didn't stop there. Your health is so important that God made your body to heal and repair itself. With the right foods, drinks, rest, and other inputs, your body will heal and regenerate itself. And when an intruder comes in the form of sickness, it will dispatch its police force, the lymphatic system, to go to battle and intercept, stop, arrest, and eject the intruder." *Single and Happy,* Godson.

God has done His part in taking care of our bodies. But as in most things, it is a partnership. We as stewards of our bodies, have to do our part to ensure our bodily health and wellbeing. Our part includes eating right and maintaining a healthy lifestyle. But a critical piece is speaking life and health to our bodies and rejecting any sickness that the devil tries to put on us.

Life is not a dress rehearsal! God has blessed you, but you must believe it and line your mouth up with the word of God. I don't care how many people you have praying for you. If you continue to speak death to your body, business, marriage, or job, it will die. To turn any area of your life around, begin to speak life to it. Declare to your business that it is blessed and prosperous. Every day, call forth new customers, profitable contracts, divine connections, and favor over your business. God has already blessed you and your business. He says in Psalm 1:3b, that if you live for him, whatever you do shall prosper. You just need to agree with God and line up your words with what you are believing God for, because your words will come to pass!

CHAPTER 2

PRAYER

Prayer is communication with God! It is the legitimate transportation between heaven and earth that enables the deployment of the power of God in the earth realm. In His omnipotence, God has chosen to release his eternal power through prayer. During prayer, the principles, mandates, and protocols of heaven are downloaded into us to be deployed in the earth realm. Simply stated, we establish the kingdom of God here on earth, through prayer.

Jesus taught us to pray: "Your kingdom come, your will be done on earth, as it is in heaven" Prayer provides unlimited access to the limitless power of our Omnipotent God. Through prayer, we become partners with God in his redemptive plan for our families, community, and generation. Through prayer we disarm the enemy and destroy his plans against us.

Prayer is a declaration of dependence. It is an admission of our weakness and helplessness without God. This is why most postures in prayer - kneeling, bowing, lying prostrate, raised hands, and so on, is one of humility and submission. Kingdom prayer says to God "I need you! I can't do it without you".

To be effectual, prayer must be fervent and based on the word of God. The bible says in James 5:16, that the earnest prayer of a righteous person has great power and produces wonderful results.

The Mission of Prayer Is To:

1. Enforce the covenant of God in our lives and the lives of our friends, family members, the Church, and nation. In prayer, we declare and enforce the provisions of the new covenant that we have in Christ.

2. Through prayer, we recover everything that the enemy has stolen or is attempting to steal from us, our families or the body of Christ. In prayer we pursue the enemy, overtake him, and recover all!

3. In Christ, God has made provision for every human need. In prayer we go into God's storehouse in the spirit, take hold by faith of what God has provided and distribute His abundant supply to meet the need.

Why Pray?

1. **God's Invitation:** God invites us to pray. Hebrews 4: 16 (NLT) states: "So, let us come boldly to the throne of our gracious God. There we will receive his mercy, and we will find grace to help us when we need it most." Prayer is both a response to God's invitation, and an act of obedience to His clear directive.

2. **Jesus's Model:** Jesus modeled a life of prayer and had a personal, consistent, commitment to private prayer. The gospel accounts show again and again, Jesus, going off, by himself to seek God in prayer (Mark 1:35, Matthew 14:23,

Mark 6:6, Luke 6:12, Luke 5:16, Luke 9:18, John 17). He prayed so much that in Luke 11:1, His disciples asked him to teach them how to pray. Jesus had unity with God through prayer. He said, "I and my father are one." In John 5:19, He explained, "I tell you the truth, the Son can do nothing by himself. He does only what he sees the Father doing. Whatever the Father does, the Son also does." Jesus simply found out in prayer what the Father wanted done in the earth each day, and then He went forth and executed it.

3. **Jesus's Teaching:** Jesus not only prayed, but He expected us to pray, and taught us to pray. In His teaching on prayer in Matthew 6:5-7, Jesus repeatedly said, "when you pray" not "if" you pray. If Jesus, needed to pray to be successful on earth, then we certainly need to pray. It is sadly misguided and presumptuous for any Christian to think that they can succeed in their Christian walk without prayer. Simply stated, if you do not pray, you will become a prey.

4. **Prayer Gives God a Legal Right to Intervene and Act on Your Behalf:** The acts of God in the earth must be preceded by prayer. God created mankind and put us in charge of the earth. Psalms 115:16 explains, "The heavens belong to the Lord, but he has given the earth to man". God is a spirit. Spirits do not have bodies and so, do not have authority in the earth. Only beings with an "earth suit" have authority on this planet. Spirits can only exercise authority

on the earth through entities with flesh and blood. This is why, in Ezekiel 22:30-31, God said:

> I sought for a man among them who would make a wall, and stand in the gap before Me on behalf of the land, that I should not destroy it; but I found no one. Therefore, I have poured out My indignation on them; I have consumed them with the fire of My wrath; and I have recompensed their deeds on their own heads," says the Lord God.

This is also why, when God wanted to directly intervene in the earth, He had to take on flesh and blood. God became a man! Today, we have a man in heaven, Jesus Christ the Son of the living God! His job description in heaven is prayer. Romans 8:34 states that He is at the right hand of God, making intercession for us. When we pray on earth, we partner with the God man in heaven, Jesus Christ, to invite heaven to intervene in the affairs of men. Prayer gives God legal entry to work and act on our behalf in the earth.

5. **Prayer Works:** We have a God who answers when we pray. Matthew 7:7-8 issues a bold and audacious claim, "Ask, and it will be given to you; seek, and you will find; knock, and it will be opened to you. For everyone who asks receives, and he who seeks finds, and to him who knocks it will be opened." Only God can talk like that, and only God can back it up, and He does!

Dr. Robert Jeffress of First Baptist Church Dallas told a humorous story that illustrates the power of prayer. A local Baptist church was adamantly opposed to a bar that was being constructed in their community. They tried everything they could to stop it, all to no avail. Nothing worked. Finally, in desperation the church called an all-night prayer meeting to pray against the bar. Not long after their prayer meeting broke up, lighting struck the bar, still under construction, and completely consumed it in fire. The bar owner was furious and filed a lawsuit against the church claiming that they destroyed his bar. The church hired an attorney who filed a response claiming they had absolutely no responsibility for what happened to the bar. The presiding judge said "I don't know how this is going to turn out, but one thing is clear, the bar owner believes in the power of prayer and the church does not."

I don't know how prayer works, but I thank God that it does! I personally have so many outcomes in my life that the only logical explanation, is the power of Almighty God to answer when we pray. I do not know of anything on earth that has the same power and packs as much punch as faith filled prayer. This is because prayer, according to God's will, is backed by the character and omnipotence of God. Dare to pray, and add your testimony to the testimony of millions who have found out, with tears of deep gratitude, that prayer works!

Delegated Authority

God has all power but has delegated authority over the earth to mankind (Psalm 115:16). We have power, authority, right, liberty, jurisdiction, strength, and ability over the earth. To put it bluntly, God is not in control of the earth; we are or should be, because God placed us in authority, gave us the right to rule the planet and gave us the free will to choose to exercise that right.

This delegation of authority was not an afterthought. It was God's express intent, which He initiated at creation. In the first five days of creation, God made the heavens and the earth, and filled them. Then, on the sixth day, He created mankind and put us in charge. Genesis 2:19–20 states that God made animals, birds, and every living creature and brought them to the man to see what he would call them, and whatsoever the man called every living creature, that became its name. God gave man the right and authority to ascribe a name to all of creation. God put man in charge, right from the beginning!

Dominion Mandate

This is God's express charge, purpose, and original plan for you and I. Genesis 1:26 states:

> Then God said, 'Let Us make man in Our image, according to Our likeness; let them have dominion over the fish of the sea, over the birds of the air, and over the cattle, over all the earth and over every creeping thing that creeps on the earth.

Dominion means sovereignty, control, supremacy, power, rule, and so on. Dominion is kingdom terminology. In his book *"Believer's Authority", Happy Caldwell* explains, *""Dominion"* is a very significant word. The dictionary defines it as "having the power to reign, rule, control, govern, subjugate, and dominate. It means having sovereign authority, similar to what a king exercises over his territory. The clear message is this: God wants us to "*reign in life"* through our union with Christ (Romans 5:17), and this means having dominion and victory in every area of our lives. Instead of being far off or out of reach, this is supposed to be the normal Christian life!

The Name

Jesus gave every believer the power to transact kingdom business in His name and as His representative. The name of Jesus is His signet ring! It entitles us to everything that Jesus has and is. When we use the name of Jesus, we are Christ's representative, presenting *all* that Jesus is! Nothing in heaven, on the earth, beneath the earth, in this world, or in the world to come can stop or stand against the mighty name of Jesus!

In John 14:13–14 (AMP), Jesus said, "And I will do whatever you ask in My name as My representative, this I will do, so that the Father may be glorified and celebrated in the Son. If you ask Me anything in My name as My representative, I will do it."

Again, in John 16:23 (AMP), Jesus said, "In that day you will not need to ask Me about anything. I assure you and most solemnly say to you, whatever you ask the Father in My name, as My representative, He will give you."

In these scriptures, Jesus, in effect, gave us a power of attorney. A power of attorney is a document that allows you to appoint another person or organization to manage your affairs in your absence or other circumstance. It confers on the recipient the authority to act for another person in all or specified legal or financial matters. A power of attorney can be general or specific. A general power of attorney gives broad powers to the person you appoint as your representative (known as an agent or attorney in fact) to act in your behalf on all matters. A special power of attorney on the other hand, specifies exactly what powers an agent may exercise. For example, you can give a debt-collecting agency the authority to collect a specific debt on your behalf. In this example, the debt-collection agency's authority to act on your behalf is limited to the specific area that you identified. Jesus gave us a general power of attorney to act on His behalf on all matters in the earth, using His name.

Jesus's name is higher than any other name. Speaking of Jesus, Philippians 2:8–11 states:

> And being found in appearance as a man, He humbled Himself and became obedient to the point of death, even the death of the cross. Therefore, God also has highly exalted Him and given Him the name which is above every name, that at the name of Jesus every knee should bow, of those in heaven, and of those on earth, and of those under

the earth, and that every tongue should confess that Jesus Christ is Lord, to the glory of God the Father.

Jesus voluntarily humbled Himself and took on human flesh; and as a man, He went even further and chose to die an indescribably horrendous death to pay for our salvation. Because of this, He is highly exalted and has obtained the name above every name; that at the mention of His name every knee, in every realm, without exception, will bow and every tongue confess that He is Lord.

No other person was qualified to redeem mankind. Nobody but Jesus had the capability or ability. He voluntarily laid down His life for us, obtained eternal redemption for us, and gave us victory over the devil, sin, the world, and our flesh. When we pray in the name of Jesus, we are enforcing His victory and commanding whatever is in opposition, whether it is sickness, affliction, lack, bondage, and the like, to bow the knee and submit to His authority and victory!

How to Pray

Prayer is simply talking to God and listening to Him. Like all communication, it should be two way. There are no special words or way to pray. Just talk to God honestly and sincerely, and listen to hear what He has to say. Jesus gave us a pattern for prayer. The prayer in Matthew 6:9-13 that we call "The Lord's prayer" is really an outline or a pattern for prayer. You can pray using that pattern. Here it is:

1. **Our Father:** Prayer begins with a relationship. You come to God on the basis of your relationship with him. God is your daddy.

2. **Who is in Heaven:** You must come in an attitude of humility and faith, acknowledging that God is God and you are not! Hebrews 11:6 states that, "he who comes to God must believe that He is, and is a rewarder of those who diligently seek Him", and Ecclesiastes 5:2 points out that, "God is in heaven, and you upon the earth".

3. **Hallowed be Your Name**: This is both a prayer of adoration (Psalm 100:4) and of consecration. It expresses the earnest desire that the name of God will be held in high honor. It also indicates a willingness to consecrate oneself to ensure that the name of the Lord is glorified in your life, home, and community.

4. **Thy Kingdom Come**: This is prayer against the forces of evil that oppose the kingdom and rule of our God. It is prayer that proclaims the victory of Calvary, enforces the new covenant secured by the blood of Jesus, and establishes the kingdom of God. It is prayer from our position as kings and priests unto God. This is prayer that enables us to walk as sons of God, and enforce our inheritance in Christ (1 Corinthians 10:3-5).

5. **Thy Will Be Done on Earth**: The earth is the Lord's and everything in it, the world and all its people belong to Him (Psalm 24:1-2). Through prayer we harness the resources on the earth to bring deliverance to our homes, cities, and nation. We are not helpless in our circumstances. Through prayer, we join God in His redemptive purposes on earth. This is also a prayer of submission to the will of God. As custodians of the earth, by prayer we make the enemies of Jesus His footstool and declare to all creation the manifold wisdom of God.

6. **Give Us This Day Our Daily Bread**: This is our acknowledgement of our dependence on God as our source. This prayer of petition includes prayer for all our needs.

7. **Forgive Us Our debts**: This is a prayer for relational depth. Here we deal with anything that comes between God and us. It is a prayer of confession of sin and rededication of ourselves to God.

8. **As We Forgive Our Debtors:** This is a prayer for individual, marital, family, and communal healing and restoration. Here we destroy the roots of bitterness, and through forgiveness, bring healing and restoration to families, communities, and nations.

9. **Lead Us Not into Temptation:** This is prayer against the devices and snares of the enemy. It is prayer for spiritual insight and discernment. That we will be like the sons of Issachar in 1 Chronicles 12:32, who knew the signs of the times. This is prayer for eyes that see in the spirit, hearing ears, and an understanding heart. This is prayer to uncover and bring into the light that which is under the covering of darkness.

10. **Deliver Us from Evil:** This is vigorous, energetic and forceful prayer for deliverance. An authoritative prayer binding the devil and his works in our homes, cities, and nation.

God loves you and wants to hear your voice. He also wants to speak to you. That is what prayer is. Sometimes, we make it a chore or a Christian "rule or duty." But prayer is really all about relationship. You can talk to God all day - while you go about your daily work, under your breath, in your heart, in the shower, as you drive, and so on. While it is important to begin your day with prayer and Bible study, God wants a dynamic, ongoing relationship with you where you communicate with Him throughout the day - not in formal churchy words or long, drawn out prayers, but even short heartfelt prayers like - "Help me God" or "Thank you Lord". Simply calling on the name of Jesus is prayer enough because the Bible says that as many as call upon the name of the Lord shall be saved! This is what the Bible means when it tells us to pray without ceasing (1 Thessalonians 5:17).

Through prayer you can join Jesus where He is at work today. He is praying in heaven. We join Him by praying on earth. Remember He taught us to pray your will be done on earth as it is in heaven.

Personal Altar

An altar is a time and/or place that is sanctified or set apart for God. It is a time and/or place where you meet with God. Do you have a personal altar? Under the new covenant, believers in Jesus are themselves the temples of God and our heart is His altar (Corinthians 6:19-2). So, to set up a personal altar, all you need to do is to establish a time and/or place, consecrate it to the Lord, make a commitment to the Lord to meet with Him there, and then, follow through.

A personal altar is a declaration of dependence on God, and an acknowledgment of His ownership and Lordship over your life. It cultivates the presence of God, and an ability to hear, and recognize His voice. Also, altars sharpen spiritual perception and discernment (Romans 12:2; Acts 16:16-19). It is a place to receive divine guidance, and for the display or manifestation of the power of God (1 Kings 18:30-39). For the New Testament Christian, an altar is a place to activate, appropriate, and deploy the finished works of Christ!

An altar-less Christian is a powerless Christian.

Is Anyone Listening?

Yes! The Bible says that God always hears us when we pray. First John 5:14-15 (NKJV) affirms this truth "Now this is the confidence that we have in Him, that if we ask anything according to His will, He hears us. And if we know that He hears us, whatever we ask, we know that we have the petitions that we have asked of Him."

Prayer is Jesus current job description. He modeled a lifestyle of prayer while He was on earth (Mark 1:35) and today, prayer is His current and ongoing job in heaven (Romans 8:34). If prayer is not important, or does not have an impact, why is it Jesus's main occupation today? If God doesn't answer prayers, why would Jesus, who knows God best, and is Himself God, invest so much time in prayer while He was here on earth and now that He is in heaven?

God always hears us when we call.

Prayer is Powerful!

Prayer changes you, equips you to win in life, and gives you victory in spiritual warfare. Revelations 8:1-5 describes in detail what happens when we pray. It states:

> Then another angel with a gold incense burner came and stood at the altar. And a great amount of incense was given to him to mix with the prayers of God's people as an offering on the gold altar before the throne. The smoke of the incense, mixed with the prayers of God's holy people,

ascended up to God from the altar where the angel had poured them out. Then the angel filled the incense burner with fire from the altar and threw it down upon the earth; and thunder crashed, lightning flashed, and there was a terrible earthquake.

When We Pray:

1. Our prayers are mixed with incense and offered on the gold altar in the throne room of God.
2. Our prayers ascend up to God from the gold altar.
3. The incense burner is filled with fire from God's altar and overturned on the earth.
4. There are thunderings, and lightnings and earthquakes.

What a powerful demonstration of the impact of prayer! James 5:16 summarizes the awesome power of prayer. It states, "The earnest prayer of a righteous person has great power and produces wonderful results." To illustrate, it gives us the example of Elijah who though as human as we are, prayed earnestly that no rain would fall, and no rain fell for three and a half years! Then he prayed again, and the sky sent down rain and the earth began to yield its crops.

The problem is that people want to see, receive, and benefit from the effects of prayer – the thunderings, lightnings and earthquakes on the earth, but are unwilling to contribute any prayer into the golden incense burner. Well, it doesn't work that way. If there are no "prayers of God's holy people" to mix with the incense, there will be no prayers to ascend before God. Determine today to contribute your prayer into the incense burner. We are engaged in an ongoing spiritual war, and if you don't pray you will become a prey.

Unanswered Prayer

Sometimes prayers are "unanswered", not in the sense that God did not hear or ignored the prayer, but in the sense that the request was not "approved". The Bible provides reasons why that can happen. This includes disobedience (Deuteronomy 1:45, 1 Samuel 15:22); Sin (Isaiah 59:1-2; Psalm 66:18); doubt (James 1:6-7), wrong motives (James 4:3), marital insensitivity (1 Peter 3:7), and so on. One of the most important reasons for unanswered prayer is when the prayer is not in accordance with God's will (1 John 5:14).

Some of my biggest heroes in the Bible had unanswered prayer. Jesus prayed in the garden of Gethsemane, "Father if it is possible, let this cup pass from me" (Matthew 26:39). And Paul prayed three times that God will take away a "thorn in the flesh" (2 Corinthians 12:7-9), but God said NO to both prayers. Also, Moses pleaded with God to allow him to go into the promised land, and God said NO (Deuteronomy 3:23). These heroes of the bible had unanswered prayer because their prayers were not in line with God's will. Simply stated, God will not answer a prayer that does not line up with His will for your life. That is good news! I don't know about you, but I do not want anything that is outside the will of God for my life.

One way to ensure that your prayer is in line with God's will is to pray scripture. You can proclaim Bible passages as a prayer over yourself and your family. You can also pray the prayers in the Bible, for example, Ephesians 1:17-20, Ephesians 3:14-21; and Colossians 1:9-14.

CHAPTER 3

PROCLAMATIONS

The Bible Dictionary, King James Version, defines proclaim as, "To promulgate; to announce; to publish, to denounce; to give official notice of; to declare with honor; to utter openly; to make public; or to outlaw by public denunciation.

In the Old Testament, the Hebrew words translated into "proclaim" are Tsaaq, Qara, Saphar, Basar, Keraz, Shama; and the Greek words translated as "proclaim" in the New Testament are Kerusso, Kataggello' and Exaggello.

The definition of "proclaim" in the Bible parallels and complements the definition of "Dominion", which is the authority to rule, control, govern, subjugate, and so on. A proclamation is therefore an instrument or a means through which a person with dominion authority can administer or discharge his or her dominion mandate.

In proclamation we use the authority that Jesus delegated to us to make pronouncements over a person, group, event, situation, nation, and so on, commanding that it or they will come into alignment with God's will. There is great power in proclamations because, unlike prayer, we are not making requests of God, rather, we are actively working alongside Him as administrators of His kingdom, with the sole purpose of establishing His will in the earth.

It is important to note that proclamations only appropriate and deploy what God has already provided through grace. Proclamations are extremely powerful when used in accordance with God's will. But it is ineffective when we try to use it to accomplish anything outside of God's will and agenda. In short, we can only use God's authority to accomplish God's plans and purposes. For example, since adultery and covetousness are not provided for under the new covenant in Christ, you cannot use proclamations to claim another person's property, spouse, and the like.

Proclamations are especially effective in dealing with the devil and the physical world. The devil is constantly at work trying to destroy God's plan in the lives of people, and he and his agents, manipulate the natural world to accomplish that purpose. According to John 10:10, the devil's entire job description is, "to steal, kill, and destroy." He wreaks havoc in people's lives, doing all he can to separate them from God's plan and purpose. The Bible states that Jesus was made manifest to, "destroy all the works of the devil" (1 John 3:8). He delegated that same, "devil destroying" authority to us and gave us the Power of Attorney to use His name to accomplish that goal. In Luke 10:19, Jesus said, "Look, I have given you authority over all the power of the enemy, and you can walk among snakes and scorpions and crush them. Nothing will injure you."

In proclamations, we speak directly, with our delegated authority, to creation, people, rulers, authorities, principalities, and things in the natural world; and command them to conform to the will of God. In Jeremiah 1:10, God said, "Behold, I have put my words in your mouth. See, I have this day set you over the nations and over the kingdoms, to root out and to pull down, to destroy and to throw down, to build and to plant". We execute this divine assignment through proclamations.

Through the spoken word, we exercise our dominion mandate to uproot, destroy, pull down, build, plant, fill the earth, subdue it; rule over the fish of the sea, the birds of the air, and over every living thing (Genesis 1:28). Jesus modeled this for us when He rebuked the wind and the waves, and issued the proclamation, "Peace be still" (Mark 4:39); and when He cursed the fig tree, saying to it, "May you never bear fruit again" (Matthew 21:18-22). Both the wind, waves, and tree obeyed His voice, and they will obey us too.

There are two different forms of proclamation prayer, prophetic and non-prophetic. Prophetic proclamations are utterances issued through the exercise of the gift of prophesy at the direction of the Holy Spirit. Non-prophetic proclamations are based on scripture. The word of God is the manifest expression of the will of God. So, when we proclaim the word of God, we declare God's will over a given person, group, or situation. We use the authority that Jesus gave us and the inherent authority of the word of God, to enforce God's will through our spoken proclamation.

Bible based proclamations are founded on the premise that the Word of God is living, active, and sharper than any two-edged sword (Hebrews 4:12). Therefore, Bible based proclamations can be offensive or defensive, because scripture is both an offensive and defensive weapon. Also, you can do through proclamation, whatever the word of God can do. Second Timothy 3:16 states, that all scripture is given by inspiration of God, for rebuke, reproof, correction, and instruction. You can use Bible based proclamations to accomplish the same purposes.

Who Made Man's Mouth?

When God called Moses to proclaim liberty to the Israelites in Egypt, he protested vociferously. After many excuses, in a flourish, he made his final complaint, "O Lord, I'm not very good with words. I never have been, and I'm not now, even though you have spoken to me. I get tongue-tied, and my words get tangled." What a summation! The Lord's response was equally striking. He asked Moses, "Who has made man's mouth? Is it not I, the Lord? He continued with a reassuring directive, "Now therefore, go and I will be with your mouth and teach you what you shall say" (Exodus 4).

You may feel like Moses, unqualified and inarticulate. But wait a minute, Mark 11:23 sets out the qualifications. It states, "whoever says to this mountain…" So, all you need to qualify is to be a "whoever" and have a mouth. God will do the rest. He will be with your mouth and give you what to say. Moses eventually said "Yes" and surrendered his mouth to the Lord. God used his proclamations "Let my people go", to deliver the Israelites from Egyptian bondage, and he went down in history as one of the greatest leaders the world has ever known, and a man God called His friend.

Proclaiming the Word of God

There is nothing as powerful as proclaiming the word of God! When you speak forth the word of God in faith, you can be sure that God will watch over His word to perform it (Jeremiah 1:12). Isaiah 55:10-11 confirms this truth:

> For as the rain comes down, and the snow from heaven, And do not return there, But water the earth, And make it bring forth and bud, That it may give seed to the sower and bread to the eater, So shall My word be that goes forth from My mouth; It shall not return to Me void, But it shall accomplish what I please, and it shall prosper in the thing for which I sent it.

Proclamations activate, launch and deploy the word of God.

The Promises of God Are Voice Activated

The Word of God is a bag of seed (Matthew 13:1-23). If there is an area of your life that is out of order, all you need to do is to find the word of God that addresses that situation, and plant it in the soil of your heart. How do you plant the word? By speaking it forth in faith.

As a Christian, you have the right and authority to walk in the fullness of your blessing and inheritance as a child of God. These blessings are made available to you through the great and precious promises in the word of God. Second Peter 1:4 makes clear that,

"These are the promises that enable you to share God's divine nature, and escape the world's corruption caused by human desires." How do you unlock the power and victory stored up in these great and precious promises of God? By speaking it forth. The promises of God are voice activated.

Proclaim A Thing

While in prayer and intercession, we clearly address God the Father through Jesus Christ; in proclamation, the rules change, and we speak directly to the thing. Job 22:28 states, "You will also declare a thing, and it will be established for you". While the power of proclamation can be released in an intercessory context, as in Deuteronomy 32:3-4, ascribing to God the greatness of His majestic name; Isaiah 61:1-3, provides a different context, where the proclamation of liberty is made directly to the captives and freedom to the prisoners. Through proclamations, we release faith filled declarations, based on the word of God, over people, congregations, cities, and so on, and it shall be established! If President Abraham Lincoln could use the Proclamation of Emancipation to set more than 3 million slaves free in the natural, imagine what we can accomplish, in the spirit, through the power of proclamations!

As a Christian you have the power to bless, and it is a privilege to be a mouthpiece of God to proclaim His blessing over people. In the Old Testament, God provided a prescribed blessing for Aaron, the high priest, to proclaim over the people of Israel (Numbers

6:24-26). As New Testament priests, we have the same authority to bless people in the name of the Lord. We are given the wonderful privilege to proclaim, pronounce, decree, ascribe, and declare liberty to those in any form of bondage, freedom to the captives, and a blessing to people, cities, and nations in the name of the Lord. You can be a blessing to someone today, by proclaiming a blessing over them. Would you?

You Shall Make Your Way Prosperous

After the death of Moses, the man of God, the people of Israel were at a cross roads. Moses, the great leader, deliverer, and intercessor was gone. The people were at a standstill. Joshua had been groomed by Moses to be his successor. Joshua was a man of faith and vision, able to fight, but he too was at a standstill. The people were on the threshold of the promised land, but they were stomped and had lost momentum. In this morass, God spoke a clear and compelling word of direction. He said:

> This Book of the Law shall not depart out of your mouth, but you shall meditate in it day and night, that you may observe to do according to all that is written in it. For then you will make your way prosperous, and then you will have good success (Joshua 1: 8-9)

God gave them the prescription for their breakthrough. The first item on the recipe is taking the word of God in your mouth! God said, if you will speak forth, meditate in, and obey the word, then you will prosper and have good success. It is important to note that this is a cause and effect relationship, which happens automatically. You don't have to coerce it, beg God for it, or fast and pray about it. As long as you declare the word of God out of your mouth, fill your mind with the word of God, and obey God, YOU will make your way prosperous.

Note that this scripture does not say that God will make you prosperous. It says that YOU will make your way prosperous and have good success. How? By speaking forth the word of God. So, instead of begging God for good success, apply the recipe in Joshua 1:8. Proclaim the word of God from your mouth!

Sun Stand Still

One of the most powerful proclamations in the history of mankind is recorded in Joshua 10:1-15. Israel was at war with 5 kings, who had attacked Gibeon, a city that had made peace with Israel. God said to Joshua, "Do not fear them, for I have delivered them into your hand; not a man of them shall stand before you." Joshua and the army of Israel routed these kings, and with the help of Almighty God, won a great victory. As the battle progressed, Joshua made a stunning proclamation. He spoke to the sun, "Sun, stand still over Gibeon; and Moon, in the valley of Aijalon." So the sun stood still, and the moon stopped..." The sun stood still in the midst of heaven, and did not hasten to go down for about a whole day."

Amazing! One man's proclamation, spoken in faith, and in accordance with the will of God, stopped the sun and moon in their tracks for a full day! Can you imagine all the natural laws and processes in the solar system that had to be suspended to keep the sun and moon in one spot for a whole day? One man, dared to believe God, and exercised the dominion mandate given to him in Genesis 1, to rule over the earth, and God backed him up! This is the power of proclamations. By the way, secular science has validated this one day "gap" in the chronology of time.

I Spoke to The Bird!

I used the same principle to keep a bird from building a nest in my dryer vent. We had tried everything we could to stop that bird, all to no avail. We closed off the dryer vent, but the bird pecked until it removed, broke down, or broke through the protective barrier and resumed building its nest. Eventually, it hatched five little birds in our dryer vent. We relocated the babies, but the mother persisted in returning to the dryer vent. Finally, in desperation, I asked the Lord what to do. And He said, "Speak to the bird." And I did! I spoke to the bird, denied it access to my house, and disallowed it from coming to my home anymore. I declared to the bird, that it will *not* build a nest in my dryer vent.

Since that day to today, that bird never again came into my dryer vent. The Word of God spoken in faith terminated its access and redirected it away from my home.

Shout to the Lord!

A woman from Australia was battling deep depression. She was in a dark place and did not know what to do. Desperate for God's peace, she opened her Bible and began to read Psalm 96. She sat down at her old out-of-tune piano tinkling the keys, as the words of Psalm 96 formed into song and flowed out from her heart. She sang it over and over, and as she sang the words of scripture, she was lifted clear out of her depression, and "Shout to the Lord", a worship song that has been sung by multiplied tens of millions of people across the globe, was born. This is the story of Darlene Zschech, but it represents the story of so many who have discovered the power of proclaiming the word of God!

Proclamations in the Bible

The Bible is full of proclamations. The first chapter of the Bible opens with a series of proclamations by God to create the heavens and the earth; and the last chapter of the Bible concludes with a proclamation of Jesus declaring His return. From Genesis to Revelation, the Bible is replete with proclamations. Below are a few examples:

1. Proclamation of creation - Genesis 1.
2. Proclamation of Jubilee - Leviticus 25:10
3. Proclamation of blessing by Melchizedek over Abraham - Genesis 14:17-20.
4. Proclamation of the excellencies of God - 1 Peter 2:9.
5. Jesus's proclamation to inaugurate His Ministry - Luke 4:16-21
6. Proclamation of an offer of peace to a city - Deuteronomy 20:10.
7. Proclamation of the name of the Lord - Deuteronomy 32:3.
8. Proclamation of the praises of God - Isaiah 42:12.

9. Proclamation of a temple tax - 2 Chronicles 24:9
10. Proclamation of a fast - Ezra 8:21-23, Joel 1:14-15.
11. Proclamation of personal goodness - Proverbs 20:6.
12. Proclamation of community service - 1 Kings 15:22.
13. Proclamation of the Blessing - Numbers 6:24-26.
14. Proclamation of a festival - Nehemiah 8:15.
15. Proclamation to honor Mordecai - Esther 6:9.
16. Proclamation of release from military duty - Judges 7:3.
17. Jesus's proclamation of the kingdom - Matthew 4:17.
18. Proclamation of healing - Mark 5:20.
19. Proclamation of deliverance to the captives - Isaiah 61:1-3.
20. Proclamation of Jesus as the son of God - Acts 9:20.
21. Proclamation of holy communion - 1 Corinthians 11:26.
22. Proclamation to rebuild the temple - 2 Chronicles 36:22-23.
23. Proclamation of Jesus's return - Revelation 22:12-13.

As you can see, in the Bible, proclamations covered a myriad of issues. Likewise, we can use Bible based proclamations to address a multitude of issues in the Spirit, and bring them into physical manifestation. When we proclaim the word of God, we employ angels, and dispatch them to execute the spoken word. (Psalm 103:20). When we proclaim the word of God, we speak through the power of God's voice, and all of heaven and earth responds to the voice of the word of God.

CHAPTER 4

PROCLAMATIONS IN HISTORY

In political and national history, a proclamation is an official announcement dealing with a matter of great importance. In the United States, proclamations have been used by various presidents as key instruments of social policy, foreign policy, and social change. Some examples include:

Proclamation of Neutrality: The Proclamation of Neutrality was a formal announcement issued by U.S. President George Washington on April 22, 1793 that declared the nation neutral in the conflict between France and Great Britain. The Proclamation of Neutrality, was arguably the first official articulation of American foreign policy, and sparked a debate about American involvement in foreign affairs that is still going on today.

Proclamation of Emancipation: Issued by President Abraham Lincoln on September 22nd, 1862 freeing over three million slaves in the United States.

Proclamation of Amnesty and Reconstruction: Issued by President Abraham Lincoln on December 8, 1863, to offer his conciliatory plan for reunification of the United States, and reconstruction of the south after the civil war.

The Alaska Proclamation: On January 3, 1959, President Dwight Eisenhower issued a proclamation admitting Alaska into the Union as the 49th state.

Proclamations in Current History

Modern American presidents routinely issue proclamations. Below are a few recent examples:

1. President George W. Bush issued over 240 proclamations.
2. President Obama issued over 500 proclamations.
3. President Trump has issued over 290 proclamations from January 2017, to April 2019.

Like in the Bible, these modern proclamations cover a lot of ground, and a variety of issues. My favorite proclamation is the Presidential proclamation on the National Day of Prayer, calling the nation to come together to seek God in prayer. Similarly, we can use proclamations to tackle a variety of different issues in the spirit.

CHAPTER 5

PROCLAIM THE WORD!

PROCLAMATION OF YOUR IDENTITY IN CHRIST

I am a son/daughter of God. I am an heir of God and a joint heir with Christ. I am seated in heavenly places in Christ Jesus. I have the DNA of God. I am a partaker of His divine nature. I have the mind of Christ. Jesus gave His life for my redemption, so, I refuse to surrender my identity as a child of God. I refuse to hang my head and walk in shame, regret or live in the past. I refuse to live in fear, worry, anxiety, depression or self-doubt. I refuse to answer to any labels, limits or stereotypes that any man or woman has placed on me. Jesus died to give me His name, authority, and identity. So, I oppose and reject every attempt by anyone or anything to limit, defraud, label, diminish, or rob me of my true identity in Christ. I know who I am and whose I am. I belong to God and I answer to only one label – son/daughter of Almighty God! Jesus paid full price for me. I will not give myself away at a discount! (Romans 8:17, Ephesians 2:6).

I am an offspring of God and a doer of the word; I am born into greatness. I am a king and priest unto God, and I reign upon the earth. I am anointed to prosper and empowered to succeed. The Lord has given me the power to tread on serpents and scorpions, and over all the power of the enemy: and nothing shall by any means hurt me. I plead the blood of Jesus over my home, children, grand-children, finances, job, relationships and ministry. I take authority over depression, oppression, and bondage. I cancel every plan of the devil to steal, kill and destroy in my life! (Acts 17:28, Revelation 1:6, Luke 10:19).

PROCLAMATION OF PRAISE TO GOD

Thank you, Lord, for all that you have done for me! Great are you Lord, and greatly to be praised. My father, you reign in power and great glory. You reign as King of Kings and Lord of Lords. I praise and exalt your glorious name, King of the universe. I acknowledge that every good and perfect gift comes from you. And I thank you for your abundant goodness. I thank you for your grace, mercy, love, favor, and faithfulness. I thank you for your protection, provision, power and presence. I thank you for my family and friends. I thank you for the ministry of Your word in my life. I thank you for my friend and partner, Holy Spirit. For all your goodness, I say thank you, Lord! Now unto You, the King eternal, immortal, invisible, the only wise God, be honor and glory forever and ever! (Revelation 19:16, 1 Timothy 1:17).

Father, I thank you, for your bountiful provisions, for the breath in my nostrils, for eyes that see, ears that hear, mouths that speak, hands that touch, feet that walk, and a heart that feels. Thank you for the dangers that you shielded me and my family from that we did not even know about. I celebrate your love, grace, provision and protection. Thank you for the food on my table, money in my pocket, my family and friends, sound mind and body; and your deliverance from all the plans of the enemy. For all that you have done, I say "Thank You Lord!" (Psalm 103:1-2).

Father, I enter your gates with thanksgiving and I come into your courts with praise. I give thanks to you and praise your name. I proclaim, O Lord, that you are good, your mercy endures forever and your faithfulness to all generations. Hallelujah! (Psalm 100).

PROCLAMATION OF FAITH IN GOD

I am led by the Holy Spirit. I am not led by what I see or how I feel. The word of faith is in my mouth. The word of faith speaks! I believe in my heart and proclaim with my mouth. I believe in God. Father, I believe your word. I have faith in you. I trust your plan and purpose for my life. I thank you because your plan is a good plan – your plan is to prosper me and not to harm me, and to give me a future filled with hope. I trust your timing in my life. I know that my God is greater than every situation or circumstance. I thank you that today your eyes are going to and fro in the earth to show yourself mighty on my behalf. Nothing is impossible to me, because I believe (Jeremiah 29:11, Mark 9:23).

I have the God kind of faith. I can change natural things with my spoken word. I call things that are not as though they are. I do not call it as I see it, I call it as I believe it. I have extravagant faith operating in my life. I speak and my faith creates. There is no door that I can't walk through because God's favor is on me. I go forth today to bring order where there is chaos, victory instead of defeat, mercy instead of judgment, love instead of the law (Romans 4:17, Romans 12:3).

Father I thank you that as the rain and snow come down from heaven, and does not return there again, but waters the earth and makes it bring forth and sprout, that it may give seed to the sower and bread to the eater, so is Your word that has gone forth out of Your mouth concerning me, my children and family: it shall not return to You void, without producing any effect or useless, but it shall accomplish what You please and purpose, and it shall prosper in the thing for which You sent it (Isaiah 55:10).

God is not a man, that He should tell or act a lie, neither the son of man, that He should change His mind. Has He said it and shall He not do it? Or has He spoken and shall He not make it good? God has commanded His blessing on me and my children. He has blessed us and our blessing cannot be reversed or qualified. God has not beheld iniquity in me and my children because we are forgiven, neither has He seen mischief or perverseness in us. The Lord our God is with us and the shout of a King is among us. Surely there is no enchantment, or sorcery against me and my children, neither is there any divination against us. Now it shall be said of me and my children, see what The Lord has done! (Numbers 23:19-21, 23).

PROCLAMATION OF TRUST IN GOD

Unto You, O Lord, do I bring my life. O my God, I trust, lean on, rely on, and am confident in You. I shall not be put to shame, my hope in You shall not be disappointed; and my enemies shall not triumph over me. Yes, I and my children who trust and wait hopefully and look for You shall not be put to shame or be disappointed; In You, O Lord, do I put my trust and confidently take refuge; I shall never be put to shame or confusion! (Psalm 71:1, Psalm 25:1-3).

In my distress I prayed to the LORD, and the LORD answered me and set me free. The LORD is for me, so I will have no fear. What can mere people do to me? Yes, the LORD is for me; he will help me. I will look in triumph at those who hate me. It is better to take refuge in the LORD than to trust in people. It is better to take refuge in the LORD than to trust in princes. Though hostile people surrounded me, I destroyed them all with the authority of the LORD. Yes, they surrounded and attacked me, but I destroyed them all with the authority of the LORD. They swarmed around me like bees; they blazed against me like a crackling fire. But I destroyed them all with the authority of the LORD. My enemies did their best to kill me, but the LORD rescued me.

The LORD is my strength and my song; He has given me victory. Songs of joy and victory are sung in my home. The strong right arm of the LORD has done for me glorious things! The strong right arm of the LORD is raised in triumph. The strong right arm of the LORD has done for me glorious things! I will not die; instead, I will live to tell what the LORD has done (Psalm 118:5-17).

PROCLAMATION OF GOD'S LOVE

I am loved by God with an everlasting love. I believe and am confident in God's love for me. I am precious to God. I am a man/woman greatly beloved. God is on my side. God is for me. No good thing will He withhold from me who walk uprightly. God has blessed me. God wants to be good to me. I am God's beloved child in whom He is well pleased. God has released his omnipotent power and deployed His angels to war on my behalf. I am more than a conqueror through Christ. God has made me prosperous in wealth and in health. God's plan is to give me and my children a good life and a great future. I receive it in Jesus name (Jeremiah 31:3, Romans 8:31, Psalm 84:11).

Father, thank You for giving me a deep awareness of your love for me. For God so loved me, that He gave Jesus to die on the cross, just for me. I thank you that you keep your promises. You promised to send Jesus, and you kept that promise. I know that you will keep every promise you have made to me in your word (John 3:16, 2 Corinthians 1:20).

PROCLAMATION OF GOD'S PROTECTION

I lift up my eyes to the hills; where shall my help come from? My help comes from the Lord, Who made heaven and earth. He will not allow my foot to slip or to be moved; He Who keeps me will not slumber. Behold, He who keeps me and my children will neither slumber nor sleep. The Lord is our keeper; the Lord is our shade on our right hand. The sun shall not smite us by day, nor the moon by night. The Lord will preserve us from all evil; He will preserve our lives. The Lord will keep our going out and our coming in from this time forth and forevermore (Psalm 121:1-8).

I and my family live in the secret place and shelter of the Most High. We find rest in the shadow of the Almighty. This I declare about the LORD: He alone is my refuge, my place of safety; He is my God, and I trust him. For He will rescue me and my family from every trap and protect us from deadly disease. He will cover us with His feathers. He will shelter us with His wings. His faithful promises are our armor and protection. We are not afraid of the terrors of the night, nor the arrow that flies in the day. We do not dread the disease that stalks in darkness, nor the disaster that strikes at midday. Though a thousand fall at our side, though ten thousand are dying around us, these evils will not touch us. I just open my eyes, and see how the wicked are punished. Because, I and my family have made the LORD our refuge, the Most High our shelter, no evil will conquer us; no plague will come near our home. For God will order His angels to protect us wherever we go. They will hold us up with their hands so we won't even hurt our feet on a stone. We will trample upon lions and cobras; we will crush fierce lions and serpents under our feet! The LORD says to me, "I will rescue you who love me. I will protect you who trust in my name. When you call on me, I will answer; I will be with you in trouble. I will rescue and honor you. I will reward you with a long life and give you my salvation" (Psalm 91).

Thank you, Lord, for your protection from terror at home and abroad. Thank you for safety in our schools, homes, streets, and neighborhoods. I take authority over every spirit of oppression, depression, and bondage, and declare that "It is well". I am walking in victory, dominion, and righteousness. No weapon fashioned against me shall prosper because I am born of God, and my life is hidden with Christ in God (Isaiah 54:14-17, Colossians 3:3).

PROCLAMATION OF GOD'S PRESENCE

Father, I thank you that You Yourself have said, that You will not in any way fail me, or give me up, or leave me without support. You will not, You will not, You will not in any degree leave me helpless or forsake me or let me down or relax Your hold on me! Assuredly not! So, I take comfort and I am encouraged and I confidently and boldly say, The Lord is my Helper; I will not be seized with alarm, I will not fear or dread or be terrified. What can man do to me? (Hebrews 13:5-6).

I can do all things through Christ. I am ready for anything, and equal to anything, through Christ who infuses me with strength and wisdom. Greater is He who is in me, that he who is in the world (Philippians 4:13, 1 John 4:4).

PROCLAMATION OF THE FINISHED WORKS OF CHRIST

I do not qualify for anything based on my works, ability, performance, prayer, fasting, obedience or service. Jesus's work is finished, complete, lavish, total, and eternal. I cannot add to it or improve upon it. I simply receive it by faith with deep gratitude and thanksgiving to God. I stand in all the finished works of Christ! (Ephesians 2:8-9).

Anything the devil is trying to do in my life today cannot be done because of what Jesus already did on the cross almost 2000 years ago. I cannot be bound, poor, sick, fail, or be oppressed because Jesus has already healed, saved, delivered, and set me free. I am blessed; I cannot be cursed; I am healed; I cannot be sick; I am free; I cannot be bound; I am rich; I cannot be poor. I cannot be cursed, yoked, or defeated because of what Jesus did for me on the cross. I stand in all the finished works of Christ! (Colossians 2:15, 2 Corinthians 8:9, 1 Peter 2:24).

PROCLAMATION OVER THE UNITED STATES

I bless the President, his family and cabinet. I proclaim God's protection, wisdom, grace, and godly counsel in governance. I declare the Lordship of Jesus Christ over the U.S Government, the executive, the legislature and the judiciary. I celebrate the U.S recognition of Jerusalem as the Israeli capital, and pray for the peace of Jerusalem. I cancel every plan of the devil to perpetrate terrorism on our shores. I proclaim God's mercy, favor, protection and defense over all the ports of entry in this nation. In Jesus name, I expose every terrorist plot and declare it null and void. I oppose every plan of the devil to attack and destroy religious liberty in this nation. Father, I thank You for all the freedoms that we enjoy. I cancel, destroy and overthrow all natural disasters, floods, killer hurricanes, fires, and landslides, and decree protection of life and property (1 Timothy 2:2).

I bless our military men and women, police officers and first responders. I proclaim God's grace, wisdom and divine protection over them. I bless the upcoming state and national elections, and call forth clear election results. I declare that I will vote my faith, and not my race, pocket book, political party, or other interest. I bless the elected president, state governors, congress men and women, and all public officials. I declare that they will receive and submit to God's agenda for this nation. I bless the US congress and call forth bipartisan collaboration. I proclaim healing over the U.S. economy, media and movie industry, and call forth truth, balanced reporting, and godliness.

I decree and declare that America shall remain one nation under God. God Bless America! (Psalm 33:12).

PROCLAMATION OVER YOUR STATE

Father, I declare the Lordship of Jesus over the counties in my State. I proclaim that the Church in my State will fulfill its governmental mandate to affect the community and society. I call forth a great harvest of souls. I bless all the media houses and TV stations in my state and proclaim godliness, restoration of righteousness and truth. I bless the legislators in my state and declare that they are men and women of integrity, citizen legislators who respect the values, faith, and aspirations of their citizens. I cancel every ungodly legislation proposed in my state and declare that it is null and void in Jesus's name. I support the sanctity of human life and declare that my state shall become a pro-life state. I call forth the Unity of God's Spirit across denominational boundaries in my state. I declare that we will love one another, and be the light and difference makers in our communities and neighborhoods. I stand against bloodshed in our streets, schools and neighborhoods and declare divine protection and abundant life! (1 Timothy 2:2).

PROCLAMATION AGAINST FEAR, WORRY, DEPRESSION AND ANXIETY

I take authority over every attack of the devil against my mind, will, and emotions. I stand against stress, distractions, discouragement, weariness, depression and debt; and declare divine perspective, grace, ability, discipline and might. I shut down and cancel every plan of the enemy to steal, kill and destroy in my life. The counsel of the devil will not stand. I declare that it is well with me and my family in Jesus name! (Isaiah 3:10).

God has not given me the spirit of fear, but of power, love, and a sound mind. I have strength for all things in Christ Who empowers me I am ready for anything and equal to anything through Him Who infuses inner strength into me; I am self-sufficient in Christ's sufficiency. God *is* my refuge and strength, my very present help in trouble. Therefore, I will not fear, even though the earth be removed, and the mountains be carried into the midst of the sea. The Lord of Hosts is with me, the God of Jacob is my refuge. The name of the Lord is a strong tower. I and my children, we run into the name of the Lord, and we are safe!

The Lord *is* my light and my salvation; Whom shall I fear? The Lord *is* the strength of my life; Of whom shall I be afraid? The Lord is on my side; I will not fear. What can man do to me? The Lord is on my side and takes my part, He is among those who help me; therefore, shall I see my desire established upon those who hate me. It is better to trust and take refuge in the Lord than to put confidence in man. It is better to trust and take refuge in the Lord than to put confidence in princes. In God, I have put my trust, I shall never be put to shame or confusion! (2 Timothy 1:7, Psalm 27, Philippians 4:13, Psalm 46:1).

Father, thank you for your lavish provision for my wellbeing. I treasure your peace and presence. I step away from wrongful attitudes that promote strife, competition, guilt, and condemnation. Holy Spirit, I welcome your ministry of love, correction, instruction, and righteousness in my life. I humble myself under the mighty hand of God and resist the devil in every area of my life. I choose to live the abundant life that Jesus purchased for me (John 16:1-15, James 4:7).

I am not uneasy, anxious or worried about my life, what I shall eat or what I shall drink; or about my body, what I shall put on. I thank you Lord that my life is greater than food, and my body is far more excellent than clothing. I look at the birds of the air; they neither sow nor reap nor gather into barns, and yet my heavenly Father keeps feeding them. I know that I am worth much more than the birds. And I am not anxious about clothes. I consider the lilies of the field, how they grow; they neither toil nor spin. Yet even Solomon in all his splendor was not dressed as gorgeously as one of these. So, if You, my Father, so beautifully clothe the grass of the field, which today is alive and green, and tomorrow is tossed into the furnace, You will much more surely clothe me and my children. Therefore, I do not worry and I am not anxious, saying, what are we going to eat? or, what are we going to drink? or, what are we going to wear? For the Unbelievers diligently seek all these things, and You my heavenly Father knows that I need them all. So, I seek first of all Your kingdom and Your righteousness and I know that all these things taken together will be given to me. So, I will not worry or be anxious about tomorrow, for tomorrow will have worries and anxieties of its own (Matthew 6:25-34).

PROCLAMATION OF THE KINGDOM

I belong to the kingdom of God. In the kingdom there is no lack, sickness, bondage or affliction. Every area of my life is operating by kingdom principles. I am an ambassador for Christ, and only the laws of the Kingdom of God operate in my life and govern my affairs. The law of the spirit of life in Christ Jesus has set me free from the law of sin and death. I have the keys of the kingdom! The Kingdom of God is within me. I have in me, everything I need to live in the Kingdom of God here on earth (Romans 8:2).

PROCLAMATION OF BLESSING

I am empowered to succeed. I am blessed and my blessing is irreversible! I am blessed with every spiritual blessing in heavenly places in Christ! All that I lay my hands to do prospers! The works of my hands are blessed. I am blessed in my body, mind, will and emotion. The fruit of my body is blessed! The blessing of the Lord makes me rich and adds no sorrow. I download success, prosperity, promotion, increase, favor, victory, anointing, wisdom and abundance into my life, and the lives of my children (Ephesians 1:3, Proverbs 10:22).

I declare that the time to favor me, the set time is NOW. The goodness and mercy of God pursues and overtakes me. I proclaim God's grace, favor, abundance and overflow in my life and family. I am blessed beyond measure. I have access to all the resources of God (Psalm 102:13, Psalm 23:6).

Father, I thank you that you, Lord, give wisdom; from Your mouth come knowledge and understanding. You hold success in store for me, You are a shield to me and my children who trust in You, You guard the course of our lives and protects our way" (Proverbs 2:7).

PROCLAMATION OF OPEN DOORS

I go out with joy and I am led forth with peace; the mountains and the hills break forth before me into singing and all the trees of the field clap their hands. For my sake, the loins of kings are loosed and my gates will never be shut. The Lord has empowered my right hand. He has opened before me the double doors and they shall never be shut (Isaiah 55:12, Isaiah 45:1).

This is my day of manifestation, there's no stopping me! The Spirit of God has gone before me. He has made the crooked places straight; broken in pieces the gates of brass, and cut in sunder the bars of iron: He has granted unto me the treasures of darkness and the hidden riches of secret places. He has set before me an open door that no one can shut. I am moving upward and forward and prospering in everything I do (Psalm 107:16, Isaiah 45:3, Revelation 3:8).

I proclaim a new season for me and my family. I declare that it is harvest time in my life. My fields are white with harvest! Father, I thank you that in this season, you have replaced ashes with beauty, mourning with joy and heaviness with the garment of praise. I call forth a great harvest of souls! I call forth the salvation of my family members, friends, neighbors and co-workers. I had sown in tears, but today, I enter into my bountiful harvest and reap with great joy (John 4:35, Isaiah 61:3, Acts 16:31, Joshua 24:15, Psalm 126:5).

I proclaim that it time of divine reversal and open doors in my life! In Jesus name, I reverse ever orchestration launched by the devil against me and my family. I shut down his operation of failure, defeat and destruction and replace it with victory, increase, restoration and overflow (1 John 3:8b).

WARFARE PROCLAMATIONS

I take authority over every attack of the devil against me and my family. I shut down and cancel every plan of the devil to steal, kill and destroy in my life. The counsel of the enemy shall not stand! No weapon formed against me and my family shall prosper, and every tongue that rises against us in judgment, I condemn. I declare that it is well with me and my family in Jesus name (Isaiah 54:17, 1 John 3:8b).

I silence every negative voice speaking against me from my past and human ancestry. I proclaim that the blood of Jesus speaks favor, grace, faith, hope and love over me! I renounce every rejection, pain, hurt, and resentment in my mind and heart. I choose to walk in love, joy, power, and self-control. The peace of God which passes all understanding guards my heart and mind in Christ Jesus (Philippians 4:7).

Father, I thank you for my freedom in Christ. Thank you, Lord, that you have delivered me from the dominion of darkness and translated me into the kingdom of your dear Son. I am justified by faith and have peace with God. I am free from guilt, fear, and condemnation, and walk in the glorious liberty of the people of God! I boldly declare my freedom in Christ. Jesus has set me free, and whom the Son sets free, is free indeed (Colossians 1:3, John 8:36).

I shut down every attack or operation of the devil against me and my family. I say NO to sickness, affliction, bondage and lack. I shut the door on the devil! I plead the blood of Jesus over my home, children, grand-children, finances, job, relationships and ministry. I take authority over depression, oppression and bondage in Jesus's name (1 Peter 2:24).

In Jesus name, I renounce every curse spoken over me or generational curse running in my family. I break every negative covenant operating in my life or family. I break every soul tie and declare my freedom in Christ. Jesus became a curse for me, redeemed me from every curse and blessed me with the blessing of Abraham! (Galatians 3:13).

PROCLAMATIONS FOR THE CHURCH!

I stand against every antichrist spirit and agenda that opposes the Lordship of Jesus Christ. I oppose and demolish every satanic strategy to use fear, harassment, intimidation, lawsuits, and legislation to stop or silence me, other Christians or the church. I overthrow the devil's counsel and declare that the gates of hell shall never prevail against the church of the Living God (Matthew 16:17-19, 1 John 4:2-4).

In Jesus's name, I say NO to abortion, sex trafficking, homosexuality, gender confusion, and hate. I will not judge or condemn, but will minister the love, grace, and compassion of God to those who are involved or impacted. I call forth unity, love, grace, faith, and salvation in the church. I bless pastors, evangelists, five-fold ministry leaders, televangelists, Christian ministries, Christian TV and Radio stations and all leaders. I bless the Church of Jesus Christ! I declare that we are the body of Christ! We are more than conquerors, and have overcome the devil by the blood of the lamb and the word of our testimony! (Revelation 12:11, Romans 8:37).

MARRIAGE PROCLAMATION

Father, I thank you for giving me the desire to be married. I know that every good and perfect gift comes from you. I know that you have already prepared a godly spouse for me. I declare that he/she is a good and perfect gift. I call him/her forth into my life. I thank you Lord that you have ordered our steps and stops to bring us together. I proclaim that you have removed every obstacle, hindrance, delay or impediment. You will help us to recognize each other in the spirit. I know that you have provided the wisdom, grace, and courage for us to initiate our relationship. I receive it now in Jesus name.

I bless our courtship, and pray that we will both honor you in our dating relationship. I declare that our family members will love and accept us, and each other. I declare that we will see each other through your eyes and bring out the best in one another. I proclaim that our marriage and home will be a beautiful illustration of the relationship between Christ and the church. The husband will love his wife as Christ loved the church, and the wife will honor and submit to her husband. In Jesus's name, I reject, uproot and remove from my life any agent of the devil, sent to distract, destabilize or deceive me (Ephesians 5:22-25).

BREAKTHROUGH PROCLAMATION

I arise and shine because my light has come and the glory of the Lord is risen upon me. The time to favor me, the set time is NOW! I declare that the night season of tears in my life is over and joy has come this morning! I choose victory, success, health, joy, peace, and righteousness because that is the abundant life Jesus died to give to me! I know who I am, and I live according to my inheritance in Christ (Isaiah 60:1, Psalm 102:13).

I am self-sufficient, in Chris's sufficiency. I call forth and create my world. I call forth into my life all the human, material, financial and relational resources that I need to fully accomplish God's plan and purpose for my life. My steps are ordered and directed by the Lord. I am anointed to excel. I am empowered to succeed in Jesus's name! (Psalm 37:23).

Father, thank you for making my life glorious and the manifestation of your love, righteousness, wisdom, and grace. You've qualified me to share in the inheritance of the saints in the kingdom of light. I declare that I am filled with the fullness of God, and thoughts of success, possibility, and glory are inspired within me! I proclaim that my way is prosperous, and you have given me the power to make wealth (Isaiah 60:1, Psalm 30:5).

PROCLAMATION OF DOMINION

I declare that life overtakes death, light overtakes darkness and victory overtakes defeat in every area of my life. I speak life to my business, job, children, finances, and relationships. Greater is He who is in me, than he who is in the world. I declare that I am who God says I am, I have what God says I have, and I can do what God says I can do. I am a winner, not a loser; I am the head and not the tail, I am above only and not beneath. I walk by faith and not by sight. I am not moved by what I see or how I feel. I will act based on the word of God. The Spirit of the Lord is in me, and He has anointed me to bring good news to people, comfort the broken hearted and set people free from bondage and affliction. I will be a blessing wherever I go. I will bring forth beauty instead of ashes, the oil of joy instead of mourning, and the garment of praise instead of the spirit of heaviness and despair. I will grow in maturity in Christ and demonstrate responsibility, accountability, stewardship, and faithful service (Deuteronomy 28:13).

PROCLAMATION OF HOPE

Father, I thank you that from of old no one has heard nor perceived by the ear, nor has the eye seen a God besides You, Who works and shows Yourself mighty and active on behalf of those who earnestly wait for You. I thank you Lord that you are working on my behalf right now, opening doors, and making a way. I look to You,

Lord, and confident in You I will keep watch; I wait with hope and expectancy for the God of my salvation; my God has heard me. Rejoice not against me, O my enemy! If I fall, I shall arise; when I sit in darkness, the Lord shall be a light to me. (Isaiah 64:4, Micah 7:7-8, Jeremiah 29:11).

Eyes have not seen, ears have not heard, neither has it entered into the heart of man, the great things that God has prepared for me! I rejoice in anticipation and thanksgiving!

I do not remember the former things; I will not consider the things of old. Behold, God is doing a new thing in my life! It is happening already. Now it springs forth; I perceive and know it and I give heed to it. God has made a way for me in the wilderness and rivers in the desert. (Isaiah 43:16-19, 1 Corinthians 2:9).

Father, I give You glory! You are able to do exceedingly abundantly above all that I can ask, think or imagine, according to your power that works in me. To you be all the glory forever and ever. Amen! (Ephesians 3:20).

SUMMER VACATION PROCLAMATION

Father, I thank you for the summer season. I bless all the families going on vacation this summer. I proclaim safety and divine protection in the air, land, and sea. I cancel every plan of the devil to steal, kill or destroy in our lives, homes, jobs, and businesses; and declare that it is well. I take authority over every natural or man-made disasters, and decree divine protection over our lives and property (Psalm 91, Psalm 125:1).

PROCLAMATION FOR OUR CHILDREN

I call forth God's plan, purpose and destiny for my children and grandchildren. I call forth the education, career, family and ministry God has for my children and grandchildren. I call forth the godly spouse God has prepared for my children and grandchildren. I cancel divorce and separation from my children's home and marriage. I call forth for my children and grandchildren, healthy male and female children. I pass onto my children and grandchildren a legacy of faith, a hunger for the word of God, a passion for the presence of God, and for fervent faith filled prayer (Psalm 112:2).

I proclaim that my children are blessed. They do not walk in the counsel of the ungodly, nor stand in the path of sinners, nor sit in the seat of the scornful; but their delight is in You Lord and in Your word, they meditate day and night. They are like trees planted beside the rivers of water, that bring forth their fruit in season. Their leaves shall not wither, and whatever they lay their hands to do shall prosper! (Psalm 1:1-3).

I declare that our children and grandchildren are the heritage of the Lord! Our sons flourish in their youth, like well nurtured plants, and our daughters are like graceful pillars carved to beautify a palace (Psalm 144:12).

I bless all the children, grandchildren, and youth going back to school. I declare that they are strong, the word of God abides in them and they have overcome the evil one. I proclaim that my children and grandchildren are taught by the Lord and great is their peace. They shall be established in righteousness, and are far from oppression, fear, and terror; it shall not even come near them (Isaiah 54:13, 1 John 2:14).

I bless all public and private school administrators and teachers. I call forth divine wisdom, guidance, and grace for them. I proclaim the name and Lordship of Jesus Christ over the educational system and institutions. I bless young adults going to colleges and universities, and proclaim that they will be beacons of light, love, faith and truth. I take authority over every satanic agenda of ungodliness, evil, and bloodshed in our schools and cancel it in Jesus's name (1 Timothy 2:2).

PROCLAMATION AGAINST SICKNESS AND DISEASE

The blood of Jesus is on patrol 24/7 in my life enforcing the covenant that I have in Christ. The blood is speaking over me and my family – victory, increase, favor, divine protection, peace, abundance, divine health, and promotion. The Blood of Jesus is on patrol 24/7 in my life and family enforcing the law of the spirit of life in Christ Jesus. I have the Zoë life of God in me (Matthew 26:28, Hebrews 12:24).

The blood of Jesus is speaking abundant life to every cell, tissue and organ of my body. The law of the spirit of life in Christ Jesus has set me free from the law of sin and death. I am free from oppression, bondage, death, calamity and affliction because of the blood. No weapon formed against me shall prosper, because the blood of Jesus is a hedge of protection round about me. Death, disease, sickness, poverty, and the like, cannot come into my life and home – they have to pass over because of the Blood. Out of my belly flows rivers of living water (Exodus 12:13).

I proclaim that it is NOT cold and flu season at my house. I oppose sickness in all its forms. I cancel heart disease, high cholesterol, high blood pressure, and cancer in my life and family. I believe and declare that by Jesus's stripes we were and are healed (1 Peter 2:24, Isaiah 53:5).

Father, I thank you that because of the sacrifice of Jesus Christ, I have passed from death to life and entered into the blessings of Abraham. I have the Zoë life of God in me. I speak life, health and wholeness to every cell, tissue and organ of my body. I declare that I have a sound mind, a good conscience, healthy body, disciplined attitude, and a well soul. I choose life and walk in divine health in Jesus's name! (Deuteronomy 30:19-20).

PROCLAMATION FOR FINANCES AND PROMOTION

Father, I thank You that You have made all grace, every favor and earthly blessing to come to me and my children in abundance, so that we may always and under all circumstances and whatever the need be self-sufficient, possessing enough to require no aid or support and furnished in abundance for every good work and charitable donation (2 Corinthians 9:8).

Father I thank you that out of Your fullness and abundance, I and my children have all received, we all have a share and we are all supplied with one grace after another and spiritual blessing upon spiritual blessing, and even favor upon favor, and gift heaped upon gift (John 1:16).

I enlarge the place of my tent. I strengthen my stakes and lengthen my cords. Thank you, God, for new opportunities, open doors, and divine connections that you've prepared and given to me. Thank you, that you have blessed me indeed and enlarged my territory. Thank you that your hand is upon me and my family. I declare that we are strong and very courageous! (Isaiah 54:2).

Father, I thank You that I am making my way prosperous, making progress, have good success, and dealing wisely in all my affairs because your word inspires the right actions in me. I dwell in safety, and I am shielded from the insecurity, economic trauma, disappointments, poverty, anger, frustration, and defeat in this world. I am in Christ, and He is my defense and salvation. Hallelujah! (Joshua 1:8).

The grace of God working in me is the power of promotion, good success, and an extraordinary life of excellence, victory, and dominion. I appropriate it now and always in Jesus's name (1 Chronicles 4:9-10).

PROCLAMATION FOR MINISTRY

I proclaim that God has made me an able minister of the New Testament, with a message of life to bless the world! I am willing, passionate, eager and excited to preach the Gospel in season, out of season, and in the demonstration of the Spirit and power of God. I declare that as many as the Father has appointed unto salvation through me will hear and receive the Gospel and be saved (2 Corinthians 3:6, Timothy 4:2).

I will be patient with people. I will not treat others harshly. I will not walk in pride or disobedience. I will forgive all who offend me today and live a life free from strife. I will not repay evil for evil. I am steadfast, immovable, always abounding in the work of the Lord, for I know that my labor is not in vain in the Lord. Thank you, Lord, that my steps and stops are ordered and directed by You. I am anointed to excel today (1 Corinthians 15:58, Titus 2:11-12).

The grace of God that brings salvation, acceptability, advantage, favor, joy, liberality, ability, pleasure and beauty is in my spirit, and through fellowship with the word, I am brought into divine knowledge, full discernment and understanding of God and Jesus Christ my Lord (Titus 2:11-12).

HOLY SPIRIT PROCLAMATIONS

I walk in the dominion of the Spirit. I have put on the new man in Christ, which is created in righteousness and true holiness! Glory to God. Hallelujah! (Ephesians 4:24).

I receive direction, inspiration, counsel, wisdom, and enlightenment from the Holy Spirit as I fellowship with Him today, through the Word and prayer. My spirit is a fruitful ground for the word. I am strengthened, energized and positioned for greater levels of glory and excellence in life.

Father, I thank you that you have given me the spirit of wisdom, revelation and insight to know you better. I proclaim that the eyes of my heart are flooded with light to see, perceive and understand. Thank you for the incredible greatness of your power that is at work in me. Your word is working mightily in me and producing great fruit (Ephesians 1:18-20, Romans 12:1-2, Romans 5:5).

I proclaim that my body is the temple of the Holy Spirit. Father, I present my body to you as a living, holy, and acceptable sacrifice. I will not copy the behaviors and patterns of this world, rather, I am transformed into a new person by your word changing the way I think. I exchange my thoughts for your thoughts. You have given me the Holy Spirit to fill my heart with your love. Help me to showcase your love and goodness to the world. Help me to live free from prejudice, oppression, unforgiveness, and bondage (Romans 12:1-2).

Father, I proclaim that I am empowered by the Holy Spirit. I am anointed to prosper and empowered to succeed. I call forth the god-kind fruit and gifts of the Holy Spirit in my life. Thank you, Lord, for the ministry of the Holy Spirit in my life, conforming me to the image of Christ. Thank you for your empowerment to be and to do all that you have ordained. I am becoming more like Jesus every day! (Galatians 5:22, 1 Corinthians 12:4-11).

PROCLAMATION AGAINST NATURAL DISASTERS

Father, the Bible says that you made me in your image, after your likeness and gave me dominion and rule over the air, the sea and all creation. I come in that authority and in the mighty name of Jesus.

I know that the devil is the god of this world and the prince of the power of the air, and his agenda is to steal, kill and destroy through this natural disaster. But the Bible declares that Jesus was made manifest to destroy ALL the works of the devil. In the name of Jesus, I destroy all the works of the devil in and through this natural disaster. Where the devil has planned death, I speak Life; where he has planned disorder, I speak order, where he has planned destruction I speak victory and restoration in Jesus name.

Lord Jesus, you taught me to speak to the mountain. So, natural disaster, I rebuke you in the name of Jesus! I cancel your agenda of death and destruction. I cover the affected area with the blood of Jesus and proclaim divine protection over lives and property in Jesus's name.

I speak over the governors, leaders, public officials, first responders and residents in the affected area, "Peace Be Still". I come against fear, worry, and anxiety and speak divine wisdom, grace, sound judgement and good counsel in Jesus name (Mark 3:27, Ephesians 2:2, 1 John 3:8b).

NEW YEAR PROCLAMATION

Father, in your name, I go into this new year with great excitement and expectation. You have spoken good concerning me! I say yes and Amen to your promises! It shall be unto me according to Your Word. This year is my year of manifestation and restoration. Thank you for bringing into my life all the resources that I need to fully accomplish your plan and purpose for my life, I call them forth in Jesus name. Anything or anyone assigned to undermine, frustrate, hinder or hurt me, I command them to be removed from my life and sphere of influence. In this year, I enlarge my territory. Thank you, God for new opportunities, open doors, and divine connections. I receive and appropriate them now in Jesus name (Numbers 10:29).

Father, I thank you for bringing me and my family into a new year!!! I speak to the womb of this year to bring forth all that God has prepared and made ready for us.

I proclaim that in this year, I will walk in my covenant inheritance as a son/daughter of God. I will exercise my God-given authority, dominion, and power in the earth. I have faith in the name and blood of Jesus, the Word of God, and the promises of God. In this year I stand under open heavens, reclaim lost territory and take new territory!

This year, the arm of God will fight all my battles. The voice of God will speak for me and be my advocate. The name of the Lord will be my defense by day and by night. The presence of the lord will make a way for me where there seems to be no way, and the finger of God will bring counsel and direction into every area of my life.

I revoke every license I granted to the wrong people to speak into my life, and declare that Satan and his agents have no authority over my life in Jesus name.

Monthly Proclamations

JANUARY

Father, I thank you for bringing me and my family into the January! I run into this year with great excitement. You have spoken good concerning me! This is my year of accelerated restoration and overflow.

I am strengthened, energized and positioned for greater levels of glory, excellence and influence in this year. I speak to the womb of this year and command it to deliver to me everything that God has prepared and kept ready for me. I declare that the Blood of Jesus is on patrol 24/7 in my life enforcing the law of the spirit of life in Christ Jesus. I have the life of God in me. The blood of Jesus is speaking over me and my family – victory, increase, favor, divine protection, peace, abundance, divine health, and promotion.

The anointing of God is working mightily in me; my life is going forward and upward from glory to glory. The grace of God that brings favor, advantage, joy, ability, liberality and abundance is in my life. I receive direction, inspiration, counsel, wisdom, discernment and revelation from the Holy Spirit. In this year, it shall be said of me continually "see what the Lord has done!" – Amen.

FEBRUARY

Father, I thank you for bringing me and my family to the end of January! Thank you for your provision, grace, mercy, and protection in January!

I step into February with joy! Father, you have made all grace, every favor and earthly blessing to come to me and my family in abundance, so that we may always, under all circumstances, and whatever the need, be self-sufficient, possessing enough to require no aid or support, having complete sufficiency in everything and furnished in abundance for every good work and charitable act.

In Jesus name, I oppose and cancel heart disease, high cholesterol, high blood pressure, cancer and any form of sickness in my life and family. I proclaim that by the stripes of Jesus, we were and are healed! We walk in abundant life and divine health! I proclaim that in this year, there shall be showers of blessings in my life and family, according to the word of the Lord - Amen.

MARCH

Father, I thank you for bringing me and my family to the end of February! You are a good, good Father. For all that you have done, we say THANK YOU LORD!

My mouth is filled with laughter and my tongue with songs of triumph. Your strong right arm has done for me glorious things! I choose to rejoice! I laugh at the devil and every obstacle because I know that I can never be disadvantaged. All things are working together for my good, and I am soaring high on wings like the eagle.

I proclaim that the law of the Spirit of life in Christ Jesus has set me free from the law of sin and death. I am free from oppression, bondage, death, calamity, affliction and lack because of the blood. No weapon formed against me shall prosper, because the blood of Jesus is a hedge of protection round about me and my family.

I speak to my soul to rejoice, my warfare is accomplished and I have received from the Lord, double for all my trouble Amen.

APRIL

Father, I thank you for bringing me and my family to the end of March! I step into April with a shout of joy

I celebrate Jesus's resurrection! I declare His resurrection power over me and my family. I have the supernatural life of God in me! There's life in my body, life in my family, life in my ministry, life in my job or business and in every area of my life! I live fully and triumphantly in, and by the power of His resurrection!

The resurrection life of God is at work in my spirit, soul, and body! I speak to areas of my life, body and relationships that are sick, dead or dying to come back to life now, in Jesus name! I declare that the same spirit that raised up Jesus from the dead dwells in me and His resurrection power is mightily at work in me.

I declare that every stone, obstacle, obstruction or limitation on my path is rolled away and I step into my destiny, identity, and manifestation as a son or daughter of God! Amen.

MAY

Father, I thank you for bringing me and my family to the end of April! Thank you for your loving kindness and tender mercies. Blessed be your holy name!

Today, we thank you for the gift of motherhood! Thank you, Lord, for the women you have placed in our lives as mothers, wives, girlfriends, sisters, daughters, friends, and co-workers. I thank you for their investment of love, care, service and tears through the years. I proclaim that they are virtuous women, women of wisdom, godly character, strength and dignity. Today I bless them and declare that this is their season of harvest and they shall reap abundantly with great joy.

Today, I arise and shine because my light has come and the glory of the Lord is risen upon me. The time to favor me, the set time is NOW! I declare that the night season of tears in my life is over and joy has come this morning! I choose victory, success, health, joy, peace, and righteousness because that is the abundant life Jesus died to give to me! I know who I am, and I live according to my identity in Christ.

I silence every negative voice speaking against me from my past and human ancestry. I proclaim that the blood of Jesus speaks favor, grace, faith, hope and love over me! Amen.

JUNE

Father, I thank you for bringing me and my family to the end of May! From the depth of my heart, I acknowledge your grace, mercy, and faithfulness towards us. You are a good, good, father.

We thank you for the gift of fatherhood! Thank you, Lord, for the men you've placed in our lives as fathers, husbands, boyfriends, brothers, sons, friends, and co-workers. We thank you for their loving affirmation, guidance, protection, provision, and faithfulness. I proclaim that they are men of valor, prayer, godly character, honor, and strength. We bless the work of their hands, and declare that every orchestration of the devil against them and their families is null and void.

Father, thank you for making my life glorious and the manifestation of your love, righteousness, wisdom, truth, and grace. You've qualified me to share in the inheritance of the saints in the kingdom of light. I declare that I am filled with the fullness of God, and thoughts of success, possibilities, and glory are inspired within me! I proclaim that my way is prosperous, and you have given me the power to make wealth.

I renounce every rejection, pain, hurt, and resentment in my mind and heart. I choose to walk in love, joy, peace, power, and self-control. The peace of God which passes all understanding guards my heart and mind in Christ Jesus, Amen.

JULY

Father, I thank you for bringing me and my family to the end of June! I step into July with a shout of celebration. Thank you for life, liberty, and the freedoms we enjoy.

We thank you for our freedom in Christ. Thank you, Lord, that you have delivered us from the dominion of darkness and translated us into the kingdom of your dear Son. We are justified by faith, have peace with God, are free from guilt, fear, worry, and condemnation, and walk in the glorious liberty of the people of God! I boldly declare my freedom in Christ. Jesus has set me free, and whom the Son sets free, is free indeed.

Thank you for the 2019 summer season. We bless all the families going on vacation this summer. We proclaim safety and divine protection in the air, land, and sea. We cancel every plan of the devil to steal, kill or destroy in our lives, homes, jobs, and businesses; and declare that it is well. We take authority over every natural or man-made disasters, and decree divine protection over life and property.

Thank you, Lord, for bringing into my life all the resources I need to accomplish your plan and purpose. I call forth the human, material, financial, and other resources and relationships you have ordained for me. I receive them now in Jesus name, Amen.

AUGUST

Father, I thank you for bringing me and my family to the end of July! Thank you, Lord, for a beautiful and safe summer! I step into the month of August with peace, the peace of God that passes all understanding.

We bless all our children, grandchildren, and youth going back to school. We declare that they are strong, the word of God abides in them and they have overcome the evil one. We proclaim that our children are taught by the Lord and great will be their peace. They shall be established in righteousness, and are far from oppression, fear, and terror; it shall not even come near them.

We bless all public and private school administrators and teachers. We call forth divine wisdom, guidance, and grace for them. We proclaim the name and Lordship of Jesus Christ over our educational system and institutions. We pray for our children going to colleges and universities, that they will be beacons of light, love, faith and truth. We take authority over every satanic agenda of ungodliness, evil, and bloodshed in our schools.

Father, I declare that the days ahead are days of rest and peace because you have positioned the right people, right place, right time and right materials in my path. My steps and stops are ordered by the Lord and I will finish my course with great joy – Amen!

SEPTEMBER

Father, I thank you for bringing me and my family to the end of August! I step into September with exhilaration.

Father, I thank you for my job and/or business. I declare that everything I touch lives and prospers! I call forth your protection, promotion, increase, advancement, and spirit of excellence in all I do. I proclaim divine favor, open doors and kingdom connections for all who are jobless or looking for a new, or better job or business. I declare that all Christians will be "market place ministers", salt and light at our jobs and businesses.

I proclaim a new season for myself and my family, that God has replaced ashes with beauty, mourning with joy and heaviness with the garment of praise. I prophesy over the last 4 months of this year, the "ember" months. I declare that I will not leave this year empty or diminished. The Lord will crown this year with His goodness, and a bountiful harvest. The hard pathways shall overflow with abundance, and the wilderness will become a lush pasture!

Return unto your rest O my soul, for the Lord has dealt bountifully with me! Amen.

OCTOBER

Father, I thank you for bringing me and my family to the end of September! I step into the month of October with great confidence.

Thank you, Lord, for your protection from terror at home and abroad. Thank you for safety in our schools, homes, streets, and neighborhoods. I take authority over every spirit of oppression, depression, and bondage, and declare that "It is well".

I stand against every antichrist spirit and agenda that opposes the Lordship of Jesus Christ. I oppose and demolish every satanic strategy to use fear, harassment, intimidation, lawsuits, and legislation to stop or silence Christians. I overthrow the devil's counsel and declare that the gates of hell shall never prevail against the church of the Living God.

I look forward with anticipation. God is on the move in my life! This is my year of accelerated restoration! This is my time, and I call forth an abundant harvest in every area of my life - Amen.

NOVEMBER

Father, I thank you for bringing me and my family to the end of October! I receive the month of November with thanksgiving. Halleluiah!

Thank you, Lord, for your abundant goodness in my life. I thank you for your grace, mercy, love, favor, and faithfulness. I thank you for your protection, provision, power, and presence. Thank you, Lord, for the ministry of your Word and Holy Spirit in my life. I grow stronger by the day, like a cedar in Lebanon. I flourish like the palm tree!

Father, thank you for the divine exchange! You have turned my mourning into dancing. You have given me beauty for ashes, the oil of joy for mourning and the garment of praise for the spirit of heaviness. I am a tree of righteousness, planted by the Lord!

I bless the month of November, and declare that goodness and mercy shall pursue and overtake me! I stand against discouragement and depression, and declare divine perspective, ability, and might. I speak to every storm in my life, "Peace Be Still" - Amen.

DECEMBER

Father, I thank you for bringing me and my family into December! Thank you for your divine protection, provision, and providence throughout this year, Hallelujah!

I receive the month of December with rejoicing. In Jesus's name, I choose life, peace, joy, health, prosperity, and good success. Thank you, Lord, that every good and perfect gift comes from you; and by the Holy Spirit, my spiritual eyes are illuminated to recognize the resources you have given me.

I will finish this year STRONG! Father, you alone are my inheritance, my cup of blessing. You guard all that is mine. I call forth and establish everything that you have prepared for me this year. I call forth the manifestation of every promise and prophetic word. Doors of opportunity are swinging wide open before me.

I proclaim that this is NOT cold and flu season at my house. I oppose sickness in all its forms. I cancel heart disease, high cholesterol, high blood pressure, and cancer in my life and family. I believe and declare that by Jesus's stripes we were/are healed - Amen!

Afterword

The purpose of this book is to open your eyes to the unmitigated power of the word of God to affect and change the physical world. This book establishes that the word of God will shift and change your world, if you will take it into your mouth, mix it with faith, and launch it forth.

An analogy that comes to mind is how lumber was harvested in the olden days. A sharp axe would be forcefully applied to the base of the tree. The first time this happens, a little chunk of wood falls out, but the tree is still standing, waving its leaves joyously in the breeze, oblivious to its impending doom. It looks like nothing happened, and nothing will happen if the process stops there. However, if the individual wielding the axe continues to lift that axe and apply it to the tree, it is only a matter of time. Eventually, one day, there will be a shout of "Timber", and that tree will fall, regardless of its size, weight, height, or how long it's been standing there.

This is how the word of God works. If you continue to speak the word of God into a situation, a confrontation will take place. The word of God will confront that situation and demand that it changes to conform to your spoken word. This is because once the word of God goes forth, it will not return void. It must accomplish its purpose (Isaiah 55:11). So, something has got to give. Its either the situation changes to line up with the word of God, or the word of God changes to line up with the situation. Well, the word of God cannot change, mutate or become ineffective! Psalm 119:89 boldly declares this truth. It states, "Forever, O Lord, Your word, is settled in heaven. And Jesus said, "Heaven and earth will pass away, but My words will by no means pass away." (Luke 21:33).

Since the "scriptures cannot be broken" (John 10:35), this leaves only one option, for your situation to change to line up with the word of God, and change it will! As long as you continue to wield the sword of the spirit, the word of God, that situation, no matter how longstanding, big, and gargantuan it seems, will submit to the word of God and bow the knee to the Lordship of Jesus Christ. It will change!

I challenge you to boldly take hold of the word of God, mix it with faith in your heart, and launch it forth to achieve the plans and purposes of God for your life!

ACKNOWLEDGEMENTS

1. Every book is the result of the work of a team, and this book is no exception.

2. Thank you to my friend and partner Holy Spirit, who helps me to pray and proclaim faithfully and according to God's will.

3. Thanks to my children, Emmanuel, Timothy, and Rhema, whose support, encouragement and love keep me motivated.

4. Thanks to the *iDECLARE Prayer And Proclamation* Team, whose partnership and hard work made the iDECLARE events so successful.

5. Thanks to my daughter Rhema who diligently produced the GraceTalk show with excellence.

6. I am deeply grateful to God my Father, and the Lord Jesus Christ, for the privilege of prayer.

7. This book is a joint effort. I am truly grateful for the opportunity to partner with you all. I am better because of you.

8. To God be ALL the glory!

NOTES

CHAPTER 1: THE POWER OF WORDS
1. Choosing A Life of Victory, Gloria Godson, Xulon Press, 2019
2. Single and Happy, Are You A W.H.O.L.E Single, Gloria Godson, Xulon Press, 2019

CHAPTER 2: PRAYER
1. Believer's Authority, Happy Caldwell, Whitaker House, 2013

CHAPTER 3: PROCLAMATION
1. The Bible Dictionary, King James Version, Online Edition.
2. Merriam Webster's Dictionary

CHAPTER: PROCLAMATIONS IN HISTORY
1. United States History, https://www.u-s-history.com/

CHAPTER 5: PROCLAIM THE WORD!

OTHER BOOKS BY THE AUTHOR

W.H.O.L.E: 5 Practical Steps To Wholeness in Spirit, Soul, and Body, LifeWork Press, 2021

Reclaim Your Destiny, 31 Day Proclamations to Build Christ Esteem And Godly Self Image, *LifeWork Press,* 2022

The Colt Story, LifeWork Press, 2021

I AM The God Kind, Living in the Reality of Your Identity in Christ, LifeWork Press, 2021

Fight to Win with Prayer and Proclamations, LifeWork Press 2020.

Choosing a Life of Victory, Xulon Press 2019.

Single and Happy, Are You A W.H.O.L.E Single? Xulon Press 2019.

Single and Happy, Are You A W.H.O.L.E Single? Study Guide.

Workbook: 5 Practical Steps to Wholeness in Spirit, Soul, and Body.

ADDITIONAL RESOURCES BY THE AUTHOR

1. The Finished Works of Christ
2. What is in Your Mouth?
3. The Unstoppable God
4. Becoming Who You Are
5. 2019, Year of Accelerated Restoration
6. A Mighty Fortress Is Our God
7. The Firm Foundation
8. The Holy Spirit, my Friend & Partner
9. What Will You Sow in Your Life This Year?
10. A Woman of Character
11. Character Counts
12. Kingdom Prayer
13. Jesus is Praying for You
14. Praying the Names of God
15. Praying Through Ephesians
16. Alpha & Omega, The God of Time
17. The Ministry of Intercession
18. The Power of Prayer and Fasting
19. Sons of God, Who are They?
20. Does Jesus Value Women?
21. What is Your Nickname?
22. Altars and Priesthoods
23. Prayers in the Bible
24. The Release of His Power
25. Solitude – Alone with God
26. Curses, Covenants and How to Break Them
27. Freedom in Christ
28. Proclamations, How Kings Rule
29. His Promise, You've Already Got It!

AUTHOR MINISTRY RESOURCES

LIFEWORK MINISTRIES, INC.

LifeWork Ministries empowers people to live the abundant life in Christ. We preach, write, and witness! Our compelling mission is to release the Life of Christ into the world by using our faith, thinking our faith, speaking our faith, singing our faith, praying our faith and sharing our faith. Connect with us on our website: **www.lifeworkministries.org** or send us an email at **lifeworkministriesinc@gmail.com**

WEEKLY RADIO BROADCAST

Gloria has a weekly Bible teaching program on REACH Gospel Radio. You can hear her radio broadcast in cities across America. For the schedule of her weekly radio Bible teaching program, please go to our website: **www.lifeworkministries.org.**

LICENSED CLINICAL PASTORAL COUNSELOR & TEMPERAMENT COUNSELOR

At LifeWork Ministries, we provide individual, family, marriage, pre-marital, relationship, career, ministry, and teen counseling. Contact us on our website at www.lifeworkministries.org

iDECLARE PRAYER AND PROCLAMATION

Gloria hosts the iDECLARE Prayer and Proclamation event. The word of God, spoken in faith, is the most powerful weapon known to man. At iDECLARE, we load, cock, and fire the word of God to transform our lives, families, and nations!

RACIAL EQUITY & UNITY

Gloria leads the Biblical Equity and Unity (BEU) collaborative, hosts the monthly BEU Community dialogue and the annual Racial Equity and Unity luncheon. Our vision is to educate, engage, and advocate on issues of biblical equity and unity; and to promote racial reconciliation and healing. Facebook@REUofDE.

SAVED SINGLES SUMMIT

Gloria hosts the Saved Singles Summit, a premier Christ-centered forum, which brings together Christian singles from churches across America for a time of fun, fellowship, empowerment, kingdom connections and new opportunities. Join us at: www.savedsinglessummit.com. Facebook@savedsinglessummit.

SINGLE CHRISTIANS CONNECT MEETUP GROUPS

For clean, fun, weekly activities and social events.
https://www.meetup.com/single-christians-connect/
https://www.meetup.com/philadelphia_single_Christians-connect/

SINGLE SENSE CONVERSATIONS

Monthly fun, interactive, Zoom panel discussion on singles issues, every 4th Friday.

THE GRACETALK

Weekly internet talk show hosted by Gloria on Sundays at 6pm:

https://www.facebook.com/TheGraceTalk/live_videos/

ABOUT THE AUTHOR

Gloria Godson is a multi-faceted corporate executive, with an illustrious career in the Energy Industry. She is a visionary, thought and strategy leader, and consummate senior executive. An attorney by training, she rose through several executive leadership positions to become a Vice President in Exelon Corporation, the largest energy company in America.

Most importantly, Gloria is a Christian leader, Bible teacher, author, prayer minister, and conference speaker. She is a Licensed Clinical Pastoral Counselor, Certified Temperament Counselor, and Professional Clinical Member of the National Christian Counselors Association. She is the CEO of LifeWork Ministries, and has a weekly Bible teaching radio program. She hosts Wholeness Workshops, Temperament Workshops, the premier annual Saved Singles Summit, the iDECLARE Prayer and Proclamation event, the Racial Equity and Unity Community Events, and the live *GraceTalk* internet talk show.

Gloria served on the Board of Word of Life (WOL) Christian Center in Newark, Delaware, a full gospel, non-denominational church, for over twelve years. And for over fifteen years, Gloria also served as overseer of the WOL prayer ministries, and is a regular eye witness to God's miraculous answers to prayer. She is a powerful minister of the word of God, with a singular focus on building lives and the kingdom of God. She is a dynamic speaker who connects with both professional and Christian audiences across the country and around the world.

Gloria loves to serve her community! She is on the Board of Faith and Freedom Coalition Mid-Atlantic. Gloria is an online missionary with Global Media Outreach, a dedicated volunteer with the REACH community outreach, the Sunday Breakfast Mission, Urban Promise, Exceptional Care for Children, and more. She loves God passionately and believes in the unstoppable power of Almighty God to do the impossible. She lives in Delaware, United States with her family.

AUTHOR CONTACT

To invite Gloria to speak, send her your prayer request, place a book order, or simply connect, please go to:

www.lifeworkministries.org

www.gloriagodson.com

Facebook@TheGraceTalk

Instagram@TheGraceTalk

YouTube@TheGraceTalk

LifeWork Ministries, Inc.

P. O. Box 56,

Townsend, DE 19734

www.lifeworkministries.org

EMAIL

lifeworkministriesinc@gmail.com

NOTES

NOTES

www.ingramcontent.com/pod-product-compliance
Lightning Source LLC
LaVergne TN
LVHW040156080526
838202LV00042B/3188